TI
TO
LEARN

**A Directory of
Learning Holidays**

Published by the National Institute of Adult Continuing Education
(England and Wales)
21 De Montfort Street
Leicester LE1 7GE
(Tel: 0116 2044200)

© *NIACE 1997*

British Library Cataloguing-in-Publication Data
A catalogue record for this book is available from the British Library
ISBN 1 86201 030 7
ISSN 0955-5374

Every effort has been made to ensure the accuracy of the contents
of this publication. However, the information for this edition was
collected during October 1997 and there may well be alterations
to the dates, prices and locations of the learning holidays listed
here. The organisers and NIACE expressly disclaim responsibility
in law for negligence or any other cause of action.

Text set in 8 on 9pt Univers by The Midlands Book Typesetting
Company, Loughborough
Cover design by Richard Thumpston (Tel 0116 270 5371)
Printed and bound in Great Britain by BPC Wheatons Ltd., Exexter
Distributed by Central Books Ltd., 99 Wallis Road, London E9 5LN

Contents

**Published by the
National Institute of
Adult Continuing Education**

How to choose your holiday using
TIME TO ·LEARN

This edition covers from **April - September 1998** inclusive.

Learning holidays at centres in Britain are listed in date order starting on page 15.

Study tours and learning holidays abroad are listed separately in date order starting on page 141.

If you have a special interest in mind

Each learning holiday is allocated a number. If you wish to look for a specific course (e.g. Photography), look in the subject index starting on page 157 and it will give you a series of **course numbers** which you can then look up in the book.

What will it cost?

The fee quoted is only a guide to the price of tuition, accommodation and meals. You may find there are additional charges for such items as materials used, boat trips and entrance charges. An **AFD** in the fee column means **Ask For Details** and means that the organiser will supply you with details on request.

Conditions of booking

Always read these carefully before booking your learning holiday. Each centre has its own policy for **deposits, cancellations** and **refunds**. These are usually stated on the booking form.
It is advisable to arrange **insurance cover** against loss of fees due to cancellation.

Travel insurance is also required for study tours abroad and this is usually an additional charge. Please check that the policy provides adequate cover for all your needs.

For people with a physical disability
Some centres have access for wheelchairs, ground floor bedrooms or lifts. Centres offering such facilities are marked with the **wheelchair symbol** in the address list for organisers.

For people with a visual impairment
The **half-shaded eye symbol** is an indication of those centres who welcome people with a visual impairment to join their learning holidays.

For people with a hearing impairment
A few centres can accommodate people with a hearing impairment.. The **ear symbol** appears against those organisers.

We advise you to discuss all your needs with the centres before booking.

A note from the publisher

NIACE makes every effort to compile the information in this directory accurately. We publish *Time to Learn* to promote the immense range and diversity of residential learning opportunities available in Britain and abroad.

However, NIACE is unable to investigate or accept any responsibility for the content, organisation or conduct of the learning holidays listed here.

Please direct all comments and enquiries to the appropriate centres. Names, addresses and telephone numbers of all the contributing organisers are listed, beginning on page 7.

Please remember to mention that you found the information in TIME TO LEARN

Learning Holiday Organisers

♿ = Facilities for people with a physical disability

👁 = People with a visual impairment welcome

Ⓔ = People with a hearing impairment welcome

ARCA = Member of the *Adult Residential Colleges Association*

Acorn Activities
PO Box 120
Hereford
HR4 8YB
Tel: 01432 830083
Fax: 01432 830110

Alston Hall Residential College ♿👁
Alston Lane
Longridge
Preston
Lancashire
PR3 3BP
Tel: 01772 784661
Fax: 01772 785835
Website:
http://www.aredu.demon.co.uk/
alstonhall
ARCA

Ammerdown Centre ♿👁
Ammerdown
Radstock
Bath BA3 5SW
Tel: 01761 433709
Fax: 01761 433094

**Andante Travels in Archaeology,
Ancient History and Art**
The Old Telephone Exchange
Main Road
Winterbourne Dauntsey
Salisbury SP4 6EH
Tel: 01980 610555
Fax: 01980 610002

Barn Crafts
St Mary's Lodge
High Street
Fincham
King's Lynn
Norfolk PE33 9EL
Tel: 01366 347841

Belstead House
Education and Conference Centre
Belstead
Ipswich
Suffolk IP8 3NA
Tel: 01473 686321
Fax: 01473 686664
ARCA

Benslow Music Trust ♿
Little Benslow Hills
Benslow Lane
Hitchin
Herts
SG4 9RB
Tel: 01462 459446
Fax: 01462 440171
ARCA

Birkbeck College
University of London
Centre for Extra-Mural Studies
26 Russell Square
London WC1B 5DQ
Tel: 0171 631 6633 (6687 – 24 hours –
Answerphone)
Fax: 0171 631 6688
e-mail: j.charlton@cems.bbk.ac.uk

The British Institute of Florence
Piazza Strozzi 2
50123 Firenze
Italy
Tel: 0039 55 284031
Fax: 0039 55 287071

Burton Manor College ♿👁
Burton
South Wirral
Cheshire L64 5SJ
Tel: 0151 336 5172
Fax: 0151 336 6586
ARCA

Carberry
Musselburgh
Midlothian
EH21 8PY
Tel: 0131 665 3488
Fax: 0131 653 2930
e-mail: Carberry@dial.pipex.com

Central Saint Martins College of Art and Design
The Development Unit
Southampton Row
London WC1B 4AP
Tel: 0171 514 7015
Fax: 0171 514 7018

Chateau L'Age Baston
16110 La Rochefoucauld
France
Tel: 00 33 5 45 63 53 07
Fax: 00 33 5 45 63 09 03

Coleg Harlech
Harlech
Gwynedd LL46 2PU
Tel: 01766 780363
Fax: 01766 780169

Courtauld Institute of Art ♿
Somerset House
Strand
London
WC2R 0RN
Tel: 0171 873 2677
Fax: 0171 873 2416
e-mail: laura.brook@courtauld.ac.uk

Dartington Hall ♿
Totnes
Devon TQ9 6EL
Tel: 01803 866688
Fax: 01803 865551

Dillington House 🔊
Ilminster
Somerset TA19 9DT
Booking Secretary: Tel: 01460 55866
Tel: 01460 52427
Fax: 01460 52433
ARCA

The Earnley Concourse ♿
Earnley
Chichester
Sussex PO20 7JL
Tel: 01243 670392
Fax: 01243 670832
e-mail: earnley@interalpha.co.uk

English Camerata Soloists
54 Pegholme Mill
Wharfebank Business Centre
Ilkley Road
Otley LS21 3JP
Tel/fax: 0113 267 5821

Field Studies Council (FSC)
Head Office
Preston Montford
Shrewsbury SY4 1HW
Tel: 01743 850674
Fax: 01743 850178
e-mail: fsc.headoffice@ukonline.co.uk

FSC Overseas
Montford Bridge
Shrewsbury SY4 1HW
Tel: 01743 850164 and 850522 (24 hrs)
Fax: 01743 850599
e-mail:
100643.1675@compuserve.com
http://www.soton.ac.uk/~dace/fsco/
index.htm

Hawkwood College
Painswick Old Road
Stroud
Gloucestershire GL6 7QW
Tel: 01453 759034
Fax: 01453 764607
e-mail: hawkwood@compuserve.com
ARCA

Hawthorn Bridge
8 Pond Close
Harefield
Middlesex UB9 6NG
Tel: 01895 824240

HF Holidays Limited
Imperial House
Edgware Road
London NW9 5AL
Tel: 0181 905 9558
Fax: 0181 205 0506

Higham Hall ♿🔊
Bassenthwaite Lake
Cockermouth
Cumbria CA13 9SH
Tel: 017687 76276
Fax: 017687 76013
e-mail: higham.hall@dial.pipex.com
Internet: www.higham-hall.org.uk
Hearing loop available
ARCA

The Hill Residential Centre
Pen-y-Pound
Abergavenny
Gwent NP7 7RP
Tel: 01495 333777
Fax: 01495 333778
ARCA

Horncastle College
Mareham Road
Horncastle
Lincs LN9 6BW
Tel: 01507 522449
Fax: 01507 524382
e-mail:
horncastle.college@lrac.org.uk
ARCA

Knuston Hall Residential College ♿📧
Irchester
Wellingborough
Northants NN29 7EU
Tel: 01933 312104
Fax: 01933 357596
e-mail: enquiries@knustonhall.org.uk
w.w.w.-http://www.knustonhall.org.uk
ARCA

Lampeter Summer Workshop in Greek and Latin
Department of Classics
University of Wales, Lampeter
Lampeter
Dyfed SA48 7ED
Tel: 01570 424723
Fax: 01570 423877
e-mail: sj036@lamp.ac.uk

Lancashire College ♿📧 📝
Southport Road
Chorley
Lancashire
PR7 1NB
Tel: 01257 260909
Fax: 01257 241370
ARCA

Lancaster University ♿📧 📝
Summer Studies
Department of Continuing Education
Lonsdale College
Bailrigg
Lancaster
LA1 4YN
Tel: 01524 592645
Fax: 01524 592448
e-mail: R.Drinkall@lancaster.ac.uk

Le Cour du Blé
67 Peveril Road
Hunters Bar
Sheffield
S11 7AQ
Tel: 0114 266 8591
Fax: 0114 268 7092

or

3 rue 26 Aôut 1789,
Escueillens et St.
Just de Belengarde
11240 Aude
France

Le Petit Bois Gleu
53800 Renaze
France
Tel/Fax: 00 33 243 06 83 86

Les Taillades Language Studies
81600 Tecou
Tarn
France
Tel: 00 33 05 63 81 52 74

and

2 Dolby Road
London
SW6 3NE
Tel: 0171 731 3430

Maryland College ♿📧
Woburn
Bedfordshire
MK17 9JD
Tel: 01525 292901
Fax: 01525 290058
ARCA

Meirionnydd Languages 📧
Bodyfuddau
Trawsfynydd
Gwynedd
LL41 4UW
Tel: 01766 540553

Middlesex University ♿📧 📝
Summer School Office
Bramley Road
London
N14 4YZ
Tel: 0181 362 5782
Fax: 0181 362 6697
e-mail: sschool@mdx.ac.uk

9

Missenden Abbey
Great Missenden
Buckinghamshire
HP16 0BD
Tel: 01494 890296
Fax: 01494 863697
e-mail:
enquiries@missendenabbey.ac.uk
Internet: www.areudu.demon.co.uk/
missendenabbey
ARCA

Mountain Hall
Brighouse and Denholme Road
Queensbury
West Yorkshire
BD13 1LH
Tel: 01274 816258

The Mowbray School of Porcelain Restoration
Flint Barn
West End Lane
Essendon
Hatfield
Herts
AL9 5RQ
Tel/Fax: 01707 270158
Tel: 0181 367 1786

Oideas Gael
Gleann Cholm Cille
County Donegal
Southern Ireland
Tel: 00 353 73 30248
Fax: 00 353 73 30348
e-mail: oidsgael@iol.ie

The Old Rectory
Fittleworth
Pulborough
Sussex
RH20 1HU
Tel/Fax: 01798 865306
ARCA

Painting in Pembrokeshire ♿
Hamilton House
Caerfarchell
Nr Solva, Haverfordwest
Pembrokeshire
SA62 6XG
Tel: 01437 721264

Pendrell Hall College of Residential ♿
Adult Education
Codsall Wood
Nr. Wolverhampton
WV8 1QP
Tel: 01902 434112
Fax: 01902 434113
e-mail:
pendrell.college@staffordshire.gov.uk
Web site:
http://www.aredu.demon.co.uk/
pendrellhall
ARCA

Radius
Christ Church & Upton Chapel
1a Kennington Road
London
SE1 7QP
Tel: 0171 401 2422

Scottish Field Studies Association
Kindrogan Field Centre
Enochdhu, By Blairgowrie
Perthshire
PH10 7PG
Tel: 01250 881 286
Fax: 01250 881 433

Sing for Pleasure
25 Fryerning Lane
Ingatestone
Essex
CM4 0DD
Tel/Fax: 01277 353691

Summer Academy
Keynes College
The University
Canterbury
Kent CT2 7NP
Tel: 01227 470402/823473
Fax: 01227 784338

Summer Music
22 Gresley Road
London N19 3JZ
Tel/Fax: 0171 272 5664

Taunton Summer School
Room 3
Taunton School
Taunton
Somerset
TA2 6AD
Tel: 01823 349243
Fax: 01823 349201

The University of Birmingham
School of Continuing Studies
Edgbaston
Birmingham
B15 2TT
Tel: 0121 414 5615/5605 (24 hours)
Fax: 0121 414 5619

University of Cambridge
Board of Continuing Education
Madingley Hall
Madingley
Cambridge
CB3 8AQ
Tel: 01954 210636
Fax: 01954 210677

University of Edinburgh
Centre for Continuing Education
11 Buccleuch Place
Edinburgh
Scotland
EH8 9LW
Tel: 0131 650 4400
Fax: 0131 667 6097
http://www.ed.ac.uk/~cce
e-mail: CCE@ed.ac.uk

University of Liverpool
Centre for Continuing Education
19 Abercromby Square
Liverpool
L69 7ZG
Tel: 0151 794 2550/6900
Fax: 0151 794 2544

University of Manchester
Centre for the Development of
Continuing Education
Manchester
M13 9PL
Tel: 0161 275 3275
Fax: 0161 275 3300

University of Nottingham
Learn at Leisure (Educational
Holidays)
Continuing Education
Block B, Cherry Tree Buildings
University Park
Nottingham
NG7 2RD
Tel: 0115 951 6526
Fax: 0115 9516556

University of Wales, Swansea
Adult Continuing Education
Continuing Education Centre
Singleton Park
Swansea
SA2 8PP
Tel: 01792 295277
Fax: 01792 295751
e-mail:
adult.education@swansea.ac.uk

Urchfont Manor College
Urchfont
Devizes
Wiltshire
SN10 4RG
Tel: 01380 840495
Fax: 01380 840005
ARCA

Wansfell College 🏢
Theydon Bois
Epping
Essex
CM16 7LF
Tel: 01992 813027
Fax: 01992 814761
Internet:
http://www.aredu.demon.co.uk/
wansfellcollege
ARCA

Watercolour Weeks at Weobley
The Old Corner House
Weobley
Herefordshire
HR4 8SA
Tel/Fax: 01544 318548
ARCA

Wedgwood Memorial College ◀▶
Barlaston
Stoke on Trent
Staffs
ST12 9DG
Tel: 01782 372105
Fax: 01782 372393
ARCA

Wensum Lodge
King Street
Norwich
NR1 1QW
Tel: 01603 666021/2
Fax: 01603 765633
e-mail: ltstudy@netcom.co.uk
ARCA

West Dean College 🦽
West Dean
Chichester
West Sussex
PO18 0QZ
Tel: 01243 811301
Fax: 01243 811343
e-mail: westdean@pavilion/co.uk
ARCA

Wimbledon School of Art
Merton Hall Road
London
SW19 3QA
Tel: 0181 408 5000
Fax: 0181 408 5050
e-mail: g.compton@wimbledon.ac.uk

Wye Valley Arts Centre
The Coach House
Mork
St Briavel's
Lydney
Glos GL15 6QH
Tel: 01594 530214
Fax: 01549 530321
ARCA

Index to Advertisers

THE ENGLISH LAKE DISTRICT

HIGHAM HALL

**The Lake District's
Residential College For Adult Education**

Amidst England's Lakeland splendour there sits an elegant country house once described by author Evelyn Waugh as "Very Gothic... with turrets, castellations and a perfectly lovely view across the lake to Skiddaw." Higham Hall now offers a tranquillity uniquely conducive to the array of cultural activities, residential courses and study breaks to which it plays host.

"... a quality Country House experience at a very sensible price."

For a prospectus and more information
phone 017687 76276 or write to:
The Director, Higham Hall College, Bassenthwaite Lake,
Cockermouth, Cumbria. CA13 9SH

Summer Learning Holidays in Great Britain

■   ■   ■   ■

April 1998

☐   ☐   ☐   ☐

1–2 April

1	Sculpture	£AFD

Barn Crafts *Fincham, Norfolk*
Accommodation arranged on request.

1–5 April

2	British sign language stage II module III	£650

Lancashire College *Chorley*
ARCA

1–30 April

3	Bird watching	£45*
4	Flower arranging	£50*
5	Drawing, oil painting and watercolours	£40*
6	Basket making with cane	£50*
7	Rush seating	£45*
8	Cane seating	£45*
9	Needlecraft	£40*
10	Pottery (any Thursday)	£50
11	Rural surprises (any weekend: minimum of 6 people)	£175
12	Woodwork (any consecutive 3 days except Sunday)	£165
13	Furniture restoration (any consecutive 3 days except Sunday)	£165
14	Landscape painting (any Sunday/Friday)	£375
15	Chair making (any Monday/Friday: minimum of 2 people)	£250
16	Bookbinding (any Monday/Friday: minimum of 2 people)	£250

Acorn Activities *Herefordshire, Shropshire and Wales*
*Per day. Bookings can be made for any number of days.

3–4 April

17	Longbow making	£AFD

Barn Crafts *Fincham, Norfolk*
Accommodation arranged on request.

3–5 April

18	Hardanger embroidery	£75/100
19	Cities of Vesuvius	£75/100

Alston Hall Residential College *Preston*
ARCA

3–5 April

20	Go-it-alone Microscopy	£57/77

Belstead House, *Ipswich*
ARCA

3–5 April

21	Symphonic band	£95/115
22	Care, preservation and adjustment of stringed instruments	£91/111

Benslow Music Trust *Hitchin*
ARCA

3–5 April

23	Egyptian art	£98
24	Astrology	£98

Burton Manor College *South Wirral*
ARCA

3–5 April

25	Jane Austen and Bath	£90/115
26	Wagner and *Parsifal*	£90/115

Dillington House *Ilminster*
ARCA

3–5 April

27	Rescue emergency care: first aid for remote places. Modules 3–4	£127/151

Field Studies Council at Castle Head Field Centre *Grange-over-Sands*

3–5 April

28	Improve your watercolours	£82/105
29	Managing woodlands for wildlife	£92/115
30	Painting and drawing for families	£AFD
31	Suffolk's medieval houses	£82/105
32	Wildlife gardening for families	£AFD

Field Studies Council at Flatford Mill Field Centre *East Bergholt*

3–5 April

33	Birdwatching – absolute beginners	£85/111
34	Close-up flash in the field	£86/111

Field Studies Council at Juniper Hall Field Centre *Dorking*

3–5 April

35	Assert yourself	£109

HF Holidays *Dovedale*

3–5 April

36	Picture framing	£112
37	Advanced malt whisky	£132

Higham Hall *Cockermouth*
ARCA

3–5 April

38	Observe and record: pen and ink	£88
39	Furniture restoration	£88
40	Healthstyles	£88

The Hill Residential Centre
Abergavenny
ARCA

3–5 April

41	Organic cottage gardens	£86
42	Botanical illustration	£86
43	Silversmithing	£86
44	Fantasy buildings (clay modelling)	£86

Horncastle College *Horncastle*
ARCA

3–5 April

45	Chinese brush painting	£92
46	Calligraphy	£92
47	Folk	£92

Knuston Hall *Irchester*
ARCA

3–5 April

48	Tai Chi Chuan	£96
49	Deutschland Heute	£96
50	Introduction to counselling	£96

Lancashire College *Chorley*
ARCA

3–5 April

51	The Romanovs: a family portrait	£99
52	History of jazz: the first 50 years	£99

Maryland College *Woburn*
ARCA

3–5 April

53	Railway modellers weekend	£AFD
54	Celtic lettering	£AFD
55	Machine quilting and appliqué	£AFD
56	How to write for television	£AFD

Missenden Abbey *Great Missenden*
ARCA

3–5 April

57	The world of Spanish	£AFD
58	Singing for the tone deaf	£AFD
59	Map and compass for walkers	£AFD
60	Painting spring	£AFD

The Old Rectory *Fittleworth*
ARCA

3–5 April

61	Découpage	£AFD

Pendrell Hall College *Staffordshire*
ARCA

3–5 April

62	Singing houseparty*	£AFD

Sing for Pleasure *Morecambe*
*suitable for family groups.

3–5 April

63	Social history of Medieval housing	£120
64	By plough and sail: scenes from East Anglian folklore	£120
65	The Cretan labyrinth: the history of the Minoan civilisation	£120
66	French weekend	£120

Univ Cambridge *Madingley Hall*

3–5 April

67	Beginner's guide to the night sky	£AFD
68	Cane and rush seating	£AFD
69	Pianist's journey through the C19th	£AFD

Urchfont Manor College *Devizes*
ARCA

3–5 April

70	Reading for enjoyment and writing for pleasure	£85
71	Impressionism and Post Impression	£95
72	Paper marbling	£85

Wansfell College *Theydon Bois*
ARCA

3–5 April

73	Drawing from model – Cezanne	£70
74	Life in medieval castle	£76

Wedgwood Memorial College
Barlaston
ARCA

3–5 April

75	Chinese brush painting – spring inspiration	£84
76	Tapestry weaving	£84
77	Stick making	£84

Wensum Lodge *Norwich*
ARCA

3–5 April

78	Understanding watercolour	£107/195

Weobley Art Centre *Weobley,*
Herefordshire
ARCA

4–5 April

79	Pottery	£100
80	Woodturning	£150

Acorn Activities *Herefordshire,*
Shropshire and Wales

4–5 April

81	Ecology of ponds and streams	£38

Field Studies Council at Epping Forest
Field Centre *Loughton, Essex*

4–5 April

82	Neuro-linguistic programming – intro	£60

Mountain Hall *Queensbury*
Price includes tuition/lunches.
Accommodation/dinner, B/B £25 per
night.

4–8 April

83	Unaccustomed as I am	£185

HF Holidays *Freshwater Bay*

84	Geology of the Lake District	£206

HF Holidays *Coniston Water*

4–10 April

85	Kilt fiction – Scottish film	£130*
86	Patrick Geddes	£140

Univ Edinburgh *Edinburgh*
**includes cinema tickets.*

5–7 April

87	Watercolour for beginners	£AFD

West Dean College *Chichester*
ARCA

5–8 April

88	Cartooning for fun	£149

HF Holidays *Conwy*

5–10 April

89	Watercolour for near beginners	£168/215

Field Studies Council at Flatford Mill
Field Centre *East Bergholt*

5–10 April

90	Small silverwork	£260
91	Landscapes and flowers	£260

Higham Hall *Cockermouth*
ARCA

University of Cambridge
Board of Continuing Education

SHORT
RESIDENTIAL
COURSES

Choose from over 100 subjects a year including
literature, music, local and national history, ancient
Greek, Latin, art history, natural history ... all in 16th
century Madingley Hall, set in seven acres of garden.
Courses are open to anyone over 18 - there are no
academic requirements for admission. Fees are around
£117 for a weekend (tuition, single room with en-suite
facilities and full-board from Friday dinner to Sunday
lunch). Or try one of our **Summer Schools**, our **Day
and Evening Classes**, our **Certificate Courses** or our
Study Tours.

*For FREE brochures please phone, write or fax to :
The Courses Registrar (Ref TTL), University of
Cambridge, Board of Continuing Education,
Madingley Hall, Madingley, Cambridge CB3 8AQ.
Telephone (01954) 210636. Fax (01954) 210677.*

The University
of Cambridge
aims to
achieve the
highest quality
in teaching
and research

5–10 April
92   Calligraphy   £229
Knuston Hall *Irchester*
ARCA

5–10 April
93   Creative blacksmithing   £AFD
94   Getting the best from
       your camera   £AFD
West Dean College *Chichester*
ARCA

5–11 April
95   Pottery with other
       activities   £395
Acorn Activities *Herefordshire,*
Shropshire and Wales

5–12 April
96   Plaster sculpture   £AFD
Wye Valley Arts Centre *St. Briavel's,*
Glos
ARCA

6–8 April
97   Have fun with papier
       mache   £98
Burton Manor College *South Wirral*
ARCA

6–8 April
98   Much ado about
       Shakespeare   £209
HF Holidays *Bourton-on-the-Water*
99   Reflexology   £129
HF Holidays *Dovedale*
100   Singing for beginners   £149
HF Holidays *Malhamdale*

6–8 April
101   Keep fit for women   £82
Lancashire College *Chorley*
ARCA

6–9 April
102   Chamber music   £120/150
Alston Hall Residential College
Preston
ARCA

6–9 April
103   Collography: a course in
       print-making   £57/77
Belstead House, *Ipswich*
ARCA

6–9 April
104   Flowers in paint, pastel
       and crayon   £144
Burton Manor College *South Wirral*
ARCA

6–9 April
105   Watercolour painting   £165
106   Photography – beginners   £220
107   Jewellery making –
       beginners   £230
108   Life drawing   £125
109   Publishing on the
       Internet   £425
110   Portfolio drawing   £135
111   Digital video on the
       desktop   £575
Central Saint Martins College of Art
and Design *London*
Price includes tuition only. Some
courses also include material costs.

6–9 April
112   Hat making for mixed
       abilities   £125
113   Papier mache   £125
114   Out and about with
       Thomas Hardy   £125
Dillington House *Ilminster*
ARCA

6–9 April
115   Discovery and creation   £AFD
Field Studies Council at Castle Head
Field Centre *Grange-over-Sands*

6–9 April
116   Japan 2000   £139
Lancashire College *Chorley*
ARCA

6–9 April
117   Painting: variations on a
       theme   £AFD
118   Lacemaking   £AFD
Urchfont Manor College *Devizes*
ARCA

6–10 April
119   Drama of Easter in music   £AFD
120   Basic principles of
        picture making   £AFD
121   Goldwork embroidery   £AFD
122   Miniature portrait
        painting   £AFD
123   Gathering thought and
        image: embroidery   £AFD
124   Bead needle weaving –
        advanced BOCN   £AFD
125   Elizabethan influences –
        needlelace BOCN   £AFD
Missenden Abbey *Great Missenden*
ARCA

6–11 April
126   Russian – beginners   £200
Meirionnydd Languages
Trawsfynydd, North Wales

7–8 April
127   Life drawing   £AFD
Barn Crafts *Fincham, Norfolk*
Accommodation arranged on request.

7–9 April
128   C19th British Art   £82/102
Belstead House *Ipswich*

7–14 April
129   Birdwatching at Easter   £209/268
130   Landscape drawing and
        painting at Easter   £187/247
**Field Studies Council at Nettlecombe
Court** *Taunton, Somerset*

8–17 April
131   Making musical
        instruments   £AFD
West Dean College *Chichester*
ARCA

9–13 April
132   Easter course:
        Romanticism in
        literature, art and music £150/210
Alston Hall Residential College
Preston
ARCA

9–13 April
133   Celebration of Holy Week
        and the Easter Liturgy   £140
Ammerdown Centre *Radstock, Bath*

9–13 April
134   Easter painting
        workshop   £190
135   Easter bridge   £190
Burton Manor College *South Wirral*
ARCA

9–13 April
136   Easter house party   £AFD
The Old Rectory *Fittleworth*
ARCA

10–11 April
137   Acrylics   £AFD
Barn Crafts *Fincham, Norfolk*
Accommodation arranged on request.

10–12 April
138   Improve your
        watercolours   £87/110
139   Walking in Constable
        Country   £82/105
**Field Studies Council at Flatford Mill
Field Centre** *East Bergholt*

10–12 April
140   Family naturalist and bird
        weekend   £AFD
141   Sketching and painting
        with watercolour sticks
        or pencils   £75/105
142   Castles – strongholds
        near Shrewsbury   £75/105
**Field Studies Council at Preston
Montford Field Centre** *Shrewsbury*

10–12 April
143   Traditional drawing
        techniques   £AFD
144   Colour photography   £AFD
145   Basic blacksmithing   £AFD
West Dean College *Chichester*
ARCA

10–12 April
146   Quiltmaking/embroidery   £AFD
Wye Valley Arts Centre *St. Briavel's,
Glos*
ARCA

10–13 April
147 Spring birdwatching for
the family £AFD
148 Wildlife sound recording
and recognition £111/142
Field Studies Council at Dale Fort
Field Centre *Haverfordwest*

10–13 April
149 Friends of Higham
weekend £140
Higham Hall *Cockermouth*
ARCA

10–13 April
150 Impressionism in art and
music £AFD
151 Learn to paint with
watercolour £AFD
152 Embroidered caskets £AFD
153 Stumpwork garden
embroidery £AFD
154 Easter landscape
painting £AFD
155 Writing poetry £AFD
156 Drawing and design £AFD
Missenden Abbey *Great Missenden*
ARCA

10–17 April
157 Trees and woodlands in
the British countryside £249/325
Field Studies Council at Flatford Mill
Field Centre *East Bergholt*

10–17 April
158 Discovering Shropshire £140/245
Field Studies Council at Preston
Montford Field Centre *Shrewsbury*

10–17 April
159 Alberni masterclass £168/222
Univ Cambridge *Madingley Hall*

12–17 April
160 Bookbinding and book
repairs £168/215
Field Studies Council at Flatford Mill
Field Centre *East Bergholt*

12–17 April
161 Pottery general £AFD
162 Oil painting £AFD
163 Letters and lettering £AFD
West Dean College *Chichester*
ARCA

12–17 April
164 Beginner's basic drawing
and painting £AFD
Wye Valley Arts Centre *St. Briavel's,
Glos*
ARCA

12–18 April
165 Pottery with other
activities £395
Acorn Activities *Herefordshire,
Shropshire and Wales*

12–18 April
166 Watercolour week £169/397
Weobley Art Centre *Weobley,
Herefordshire*
ARCA

13–17 April
167 Painting and stitching
felt £150/200
Alston Hall Residential College
Preston
ARCA

13–17 April
168 Gannets galore (YOC) £AFD
Field Studies Council at Dale Fort
Field Centre *Haverfordwest*

13–17 April
169 Rescue emergency care:
first aid for remote
places – Modules 1–4 £238/288
Field Studies Council at Castle Head
Field Centre *Grange-over-Sands*

13–17 April
170 Drawing next step £179
HF Holidays *Whitby*

21

13–17 April

171	The London music hall	£AFD
172	Learn to paint with watercolour	£AFD
173	3-D Découpage	£AFD
174	Drawing and painting for the petrified	£AFD
175	C & G hat making – beginners	£AFD
176	Silk ribbon embroidery BOCN	£AFD
177	Painting techniques – BOCN	£AFD

Missenden Abbey *Great Missenden*
ARCA

13–17 April

178	Drawing and painting: surface as subject	£240

Univ Cambridge *Madingley Hall*

13–19 April

179	Baroque opera project	£267/307

Benslow Music Trust *Hitchin*
ARCA

14–15 April

180	Sculpture	£AFD

Barn Crafts *Fincham, Norfolk*
Accommodation arranged on request.

14–16 April

181	Aromatherapy for family and friends	£98
182	Enamelling for everyone	£98

Burton Manor College *South Wirral*
ARCA

14–16 April

183	Dollmaking	£125
184	Living in the past	£105/120
185	Painting on china in the French style	£125

Dillington House *Ilminster*
ARCA

14–16 April

186	Beaded bags and tassels	£AFD

West Dean College *Chichester*
ARCA

14–16 April

187	Bridge: The Fundamentals	£75/95

Belstead House *Ipswich*
ARCA

14–17 April

188	Fashion design	£150
189	Graphic design	£150
190	Figure drawing	£125
191	Paper making	£130
192	Apple Mac – beginners	£440
193	Fine print	£220
194	Etching	£145
195	Pattern cutting workshop	£230
196	Premiere and after effects – beginners	£425

Central Saint Martins College of Art and Design *London*
Price includes tuition only. Some courses also include material costs.

14–17 April

197	A level revision course in French, Spanish and German	£195

Lancashire College *Chorley*
ARCA

14–17 April

198	Hand spinning linen	£AFD
199	Batik and indigo dyeing	£AFD
200	Painting flowers in water colour	£AFD

Urchfont Manor College *Devizes*
ARCA

14–17 April

201	Early music for recorder	£111
202	Singing together	£111

Wedgwood Memorial College *Barlaston*
ARCA

15–17 April

203	Découpage	£82

Lancashire College *Chorley*
ARCA

15–18 April

204	Bridge	£175

Hawthorn Bridge *Tiverton, Devon*

15–19 April
205   Dartington Hall Easter
        Conference: Learning for
        sustainable living   £AFD
Dartington Hall *Totnes, Devon*

16–19 April
206   Develop your Bridge   £113/143
Belstead House *Ipswich*
ARCA

17–18 April
207   Interior design on a
        budget   £AFD
Barn Crafts *Fincham, Norfolk*
Accommodation arranged on request.

17–19 April
208   Tracing family history   £75/100
209   Speed appliqué methods £75/100
Alston Hall Residential College
Preston
ARCA

17–19 April
210   American line dancing   £98
211   Talking with confidence   £98
Burton Manor College *South Wirral*
ARCA

17–19 April
212   Second Haworth
        Chamber Music
        Weekend (concerts,
        ensemble coaching and
        individual training)   £AFD
English Camerata Soloists *Haworth,
West Yorkshire*

17–19 April
213   Southern Lake District:
        geology and history   £80/104
Field Studies Council at Castle Head
Field Centre *Grange-over-Sands*

17–19 April
214   Gardening for wildlife   £82/105
215   Otters and other
        riverside mammals   £82/105
216   Wildlife watch for
        families   £AFD
Field Studies Council at Flatford Mill
Field Centre *East Bergholt*

17–19 April
217   Birds of ley and coast   £79/105
218   Plants and magnifers:
        resources for teaching   £75/100
Field Studies Council at Slapton Ley
Field Centre *Kingsbridge, Devon*

17–19 April
219   Hawkwood Chamber
        Orchestra   £94/122
Hawkwood College *Stroud, Glos*
ARCA

17–19 April
220   Wine appreciation   £194
HF Holidays *Abingworth*
221   Industrial heritage of
        South Wales   £179
HF Holidays *Brecon*
222   Yoga   £124
HF Holidays *Thurlestone Sands*
223   Music making for
        beginners   £169
HF Holidays *Malhamdale*

17–19 April
224   Chinese brush painting   £88
225   Somerset churches   £98
226   Découpage   £68
The Hill Residential Centre
Abergavenny
ARCA

17–19 April
227   Reiki healing   £92
228   Lacemaking for all   £92
229   Boost your confidence   £92
230   Canal boat art   £92
231   Egyptian art   £92
Knuston Hall *Irchester*
ARCA

17–19 April
232   Ruskin linen   £96
233   Batik   £96
234   Numerology – power key
        to life   £96
235   Drama   £96
Lancashire College *Chorley*
ARCA

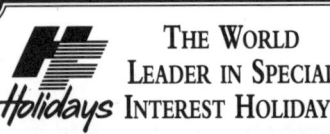

17–19 April
236 Rise and fall of the
Knights Templar £99
237 Batik textiles £99
Maryland College *Woburn*
ARCA

17–19 April
238 Basic china mending £135
Mowbray School of Porcelain
Restoration *Hatfield, Herts*

17–19 April
239 Watercolour workshop £AFD
240 Alexander Technique £AFD
241 Let's dance – a weekend
for recorder players £AFD
242 Why pay more for your
wines? £AFD
The Old Rectory *Fittleworth*
ARCA

17–19 April
243 Art and the Greeks £120
244 Geology of East Anglia £120
245 Books of hours and
songs of courtly love £120
246 Medieval mysteries £120
Univ Cambridge *Madingley Hall*

17–19 April
247 Victorian popular cultures £AFD
248 Spring into words £AFD
Urchfont Manor College *Devizes*
ARCA

17–19 April
249 Health studies: the
human body £85
250 Italian – advanced £91
Wansfell College *Theydon Bois*
ARCA

17–19 April
251 Stained glass £AFD
252 Batik on fabric and paper £AFD
253 Silversmithing –
introduction £AFD
254 Botanical illustration £AFD
255 Calligraphy – illuminated
miniature £AFD
West Dean College *Chichester*
ARCA

17–19 April
256 Studying stained glass £AFD
Wye Valley Arts Centre *St. Briavel's,*
Glos
ARCA

17–20 April
257 Drawing and painting on
silk £AFD
West Dean College *Chichester*
ARCA

17–21 April
258 Stone carving workshop £AFD
West Dean College *Chichester*
ARCA

17–24 April
259 Watercolour painting £AFD
Wye Valley Arts Centre *St. Briavel's,*
Glos
ARCA

18–19 April
260 Gourmet cooking £120
261 Garden design £100
262 Drawing for the terrified £96
263 Stained glass £120
Acorn Activities *Herefordshire,*
Shropshire and Wales

18–19 April
264 Sculpture £AFD
Barn Crafts *Fincham, Norfolk*
Accommodation arranged on request.

18–19 April
265 Belly dancing £60
Mountain Hall *Queensbury*
Price includes tuition/lunches.
Accommodation/dinner, B/B £25 per
night.

19–24 April
266 Botanical illustration £260
Higham Hall *Cockermouth*
ARCA

19–24 April
267 Bookbinding £AFD
West Dean College *Chichester*
ARCA

19–25 April
268   Pots and flowers in
      watercolour   £169/397
Weobley Art Centre *Weobley,*
Herefordshire
ARCA

20–22 April
269   Canvas work   £82
270   Yoga   £82
Lancashire College *Chorley*
ARCA

20–23 April
271   Calligraphy – Gothic
      blackletter   £209
HF Holidays *Abingworth*

20–23 April
272   Certificate in the theory
      of counselling –
      humanistic/person-centred
      counselling – the theory   £139
Lancashire College *Chorley*
ARCA

20–24 April
273   Quilting techniques from
      India   £AFD
274   Exploring mixed media   £AFD
275   Spring birds and wildlife   £AFD
The Old Rectory *Fittleworth*
ARCA

20–24 April
276   Glorious gardens –
      historic houses   £170
Wedgwood Memorial College
Barlaston
ARCA

20–25 April
277   Lacemaking   £AFD
Dartington Hall *Totnes, Devon*

21–22 April
278   Embroidery – without
      kits   £AFD
Barn Crafts *Fincham, Norfolk*
Accommodation arranged on request.

22–24 April
279   Take your pencil for a
      walk   £AFD
Pendrell Hall College *Staffordshire*
ARCA

23–26 April
280   Silversmithing   £120
281   Before the A40   £98
282   Advanced French   £88
283   Floral art   £88
The Hill Residential Centre
Abergavenny
ARCA

24–25 April
284   Watercolour painting on
      location   £AFD
Barn Crafts *Fincham, Norfolk*
Accommodation arranged on request.

24–26 April
285   Japanese embroidery   £75/100
286   Writing for TV   £75/100
Alston Hall Residential College
Preston
ARCA

24–26 April
287   Bucks Point and Floral
      Torchon Lace   £75/95
Belstead House *Ipswich*
ARCA

24–26 April
288   Discovering geology   £98
289   Photography – black and
      white printing   £170
Burton Manor College *South Wirral*
ARCA

24–26 April
290   Ancient Egyptian religion £79/105
291   Buddhism and
      philosophy   £79/105
292   Upstairs, downstairs –
      life in the English country
      house   £85/110
Dillington House *Ilminster*
ARCA

24–26 April

_293_	National Vegetation Classification (NVC)	£92/115
_294_	Painting spring flowers	£82/105
_295_	Spring wild flower weekend	£82/105

Field Studies Council at Flatford Mill Field Centre _East Bergholt_

24–26 April

_296_	Identifying freshwater invertebrates	£78/102

Field Studies Council at Juniper Hall Field Centre _Dorking_

24–26 April

_297_	Sphagnum weekend	£100/122

Field Studies Council at Rhyd-y-creuau _Betws-y-coed_

24–26 April

_298_	Beginner's guide to the camcorder	£112
_299_	Willow sculpture	£112

Higham Hall _Cockermouth_
ARCA

24–26 April

_300_	Baskets, boxes and bunches (flower arranging)	£86
_301_	Aviation	£96

Horncastle College _Horncastle_
ARCA

24–26 April

_302_	C & G lace – I and II	£83
_303_	Hand colouring black and white photographs	£92
_304_	Painting on silk and other natural fabrics	£92
_305_	Spanish literature	£92

Knuston Hall _Irchester_
ARCA

24–26 April

_306_	Portuguese	£96
_307_	Flower painting in watercolour	£96
_308_	Assertiveness training	£96
_309_	Modelling salt dough	£96

Lancashire College _Chorley_
ARCA

24–26 April

_310_	George Sand – Romans Champêtres	£99

Maryland College _Woburn_
ARCA

24–26 April

_311_	Use of poetry and song in learning Russian	£70

Meirionnydd Languages
Trawsfynydd, North Wales

24–26 April

_312_	The song recital	£AFD
_313_	Floats as decoration – textile design	£AFD
_314_	Bridge – improve your declarer play and all about Stayman	£AFD
_315_	Art decoded: C17th and C18th	£AFD
_316_	Nature's awakening	£AFD
_317_	The Jazz Age in literature	£AFD
_318_	Machine embroidery BOCN	£AFD

Missenden Abbey _Great Missenden_
ARCA

24–26 April

_319_	How to be a travel writer	£AFD
_320_	Beautiful batik	£AFD
_321_	Sunlight in landscape in watercolour	£AFD
_322_	Walking the Downs and Weald	£AFD

The Old Rectory _Fittleworth_
ARCA

24–26 April

_323_	Landscape painting	£185

Painting in Pembrokeshire _St. David's_

24–26 April

_324_	Calligraphy	£AFD
_325_	China painting	£AFD
_326_	Lacemaking	£AFD

Pendrell Hall College _Staffordshire_
ARCA

24–26 April

_327_	Richard III: good or bad?	£129

Univ Birmingham _Ludlow, Shropshire_

24–26 April
328	Reading Latin	£120
329	Jazz weekend	£120
330	D H Lawrence and E M Forster	£120
331	World religions: an introductory experience	£120

Univ Cambridge *Madingley Hall*

24–26 April
332	The geology around Llandrindod Wells	£AFD

Univ Liverpool *Llandrindod Wells*

24–26 April
333	Decorative stained glass	£AFD
334	Alexander Technique	£AFD
335	Medieval women	£AFD

Urchfont Manor College *Devizes*
ARCA

24–26 April
336	The piano and the voice	£85
337	Photography: advanced monichrome printing	£102

Wansfell College *Theydon Bois*
ARCA

24–26 April
338	Conversational Spanish	£70
339	Josiah Wedgwood and the Neoclassical ideal	£70

Wedgwood Memorial College
Barlaston
ARCA

24–26 April
340	Memoir writing	£84
341	Garden sculpture	£84
342	George Gershwin celebration	£84

Wensum Lodge *Norwich*
ARCA

24–26 April .
343	Mounting and framing pictures	£AFD
344	Creative watercolour – beginners	£AFD
345	Cabinet making – part 1	£AFD
346	Getting started with watercolour	£AFD
347	General silversmithing	£AFD

West Dean College *Chichester*
ARCA

24–26 April
348	Monoprinting	£AFD
349	Studying the Hereford School of Sculpture	£AFD

Wye Valley Arts Centre *St. Briavel's, Glos*
ARCA

24–27 April
350	Exploring country houses near Banbury	£399

Univ Birmingham *Banbury, Oxfordshire*

24–27 April
351	Low relief and chip carving in wood	£AFD

West Dean College *Chichester*
ARCA

24 April–1 May
352	Surrey woodlands: their history and ecology	£238/280

Field Studies Council at Juniper Hall
Field Centre *Dorking*

25–26 April
353	Silversmithing and jewellery	£120

Acorn Activities *Herefordshire, Shropshire and Wales*

25–26 April
354	Woodland ecoiogy and management	£38

Field Studies Council at Epping Forest
Field Centre *Loughton, Essex*

25–26 April
355	Psychic awareness	£60

Mountain Hall *Queensbury*
Price includes tuition/lunches. Accommodation/dinner, B/B £25 per night.

25–26 April
356	England and France in Medieval times	£AFD

Univ Manchester *Manchester*

25–29 April
357	Sea shore studies in Looe	£220

Univ Wales, Swansea *Looe, Cornwall*

26 April–1 May
358   Wet into wet
        watercolour   £260
Higham Hall *Cockermouth*
ARCA

26 April–1 May
359   Beginners' life drawing   £AFD
360   Malachite and
        marbling/paint effects   £AFD
Wye Valley Arts Centre *St. Briavel's,
Glos*
ARCA

27–29 April
361   Alexander Technique   £80/100
Alston Hall Residential College
Preston
ARCA

27–29 April
362   Stamping for pleasure
        and profit   £82
363   Film studies   £82
364   Introduction to clay
        modelling – 3D sculpture   £82
Lancashire College *Chorley*
ARCA

27–29 April
365   Fruit and flowers: still life
        from Greeks to Picasso   £85
Wansfell College *Theydon Bois*
ARCA

27–30 April
366   Recorder rendezvous   £115/140
Benslow Music Trust *Hitchin*
ARCA

27 April–1 May
367   From steam engines to
        microchips   £170
Wansfell College *Theydon Bois*
ARCA

27 April–2 May
368   Porcelain restoration –
        beginners   £235
Mowbray School of Porcelain
Restoration *Hatfield, Herts*

29 April–6 May
369   Mosses and liverworts £198/255
Field Studies Council at Orielton Field
Centre *Pembroke*

■   ■   ■   ■

May 1998

☐   ☐   ☐   ☐

tba
370   Study weekend at
        Stoneyhurst College   £AFD
Univ Liverpool *Clitheroe, Lancashire*

1–2 May
371   Interior design on a
        budget   £AFD
Barn Crafts *Fincham, Norfolk*
Accommodation arranged on request.

1–3 May
372   Bedfordshire lace   £75/100
373   Chamber choir weekend £75/100
Alston Hall Residential College
Preston
ARCA

1–3 May
374   Suffolk and the world: a
        local history course   £78/98
Belstead House *Ipswich*
ARCA

1–3 May
375   The intermediate cellist   £87/107
376   The flute weekend   £91/111
Benslow Music Trust *Hitchin*
ARCA

1–3 May
377   Hand painted furniture   £98
Burton Manor College *South Wirral*
ARCA

1–3 May
378   Playing the recorder –
        from Ghizeghem to
        Gerschwin   £79/105
Dillington House *Ilminster*
ARCA

1–3 May
379   Lichens near London   £89/115
Field Studies Council at Juniper Hall
Field Centre *Dorking*

1–3 May
380   Bird song   £75/105
381   Badgers   £75/105
Field Studies Council at Preston
Montford Field Centre *Shrewsbury*

1–3 May
382   Elgar in the Dales   £179
HF Holidays *Malhamdale*

1–3 May
383   *Don Giovanni*   £88
384   Architectural clues   £88
385   Patchwork and quilting   £88
386   Advanced bridge   £88
The Hill Residential Centre
Abergavenny
ARCA

1–3 May
387   Life and landscape
        painting   £94
388   China painting   £86
389   Bridge   £86
390   Continental lacemaking   £86
Horncastle College *Horncastle*
ARCA

1–3 May
391   Embroidery   £92
392   Gold weekend   £92
393   Introducing N.L.P.   £92
394   Creative writing
        workshop   £92
Knuston Hall *Irchester*
ARCA

1–3 May
395   German   £96
396   Introduction to
        aromatherapy   £96
397   Inventing, inventors and
        inventions   £96
Lancashire College *Chorley*
ARCA

1–3 May
398   Alexander Technique   £99
399   The medicinal use of
        herbs   £99
400   Japanese ceramics   £99
Maryland College *Woburn*
ARCA

1–3 May
401   Magritte   £AFD
402   Many coloured wines
        from Mediterranean
        regions   £AFD
403   World of gemstones   £AFD
404   Be your own financial
        adviser   £AFD
405   Danté – introduction   £AFD
406   Keyboarding leisure play
        – intermediate   £AFD
407   C & G patchwork and
        quilting   £AFD
Missenden Abbey *Great Missenden*
ARCA

1–3 May
408   Painting water and
        reflections   £AFD
409   Harpsichord workshop   £AFD
410   Chinese brush painting   £AFD
The Old Rectory *Fittleworth*
ARCA

1–3 May
411   Life painting   £AFD
412   Video editing   £AFD
413   English music   £AFD
Pendrell Hall College *Staffs*
ARCA

1–3 May

414	Great instrumentalists of the past	£120
415	C18th art in England	£120
416	History of architecture: Medieval cities	£120
417	Theory and practice of archaeological illustration	£120

Univ Cambridge *Madingley Hall*

1–3 May

418	Piping and drumming weekend	£AFD

Urchfont Manor College *Devizes*
ARCA

1–3 May

419	Anglo Saxon literature	£85
420	Learn to play the mandolin in a weekend	£85
421	Music for mandolin ensemble	£85

Wansfell College *Theydon Bois*
ARCA

1–3 May

422	Deutsch Aktiv	£76
423	Joan of Arc	£63

Wedgwood Memorial College
Barlaston
ARCA

1–3 May

424	Pottery – throwing and turning	£AFD
425	Wood engraving	£AFD
426	Still life with flowers in oils	£AFD
427	Watercolour for beginners	£AFD
428	Jewellery making	£AFD
429	Tradition with a twist – machine quilting	£AFD
430	Woodturning	£AFD

West Dean College *Chichester*
ARCA

1–4 May

431	Painting and drawing miniatures	£108/140
432	RPS Nature Group field weekend and distinctions workshop	£120/155

Field Studies Council at Juniper Hall
Field Centre *Dorking*

1–4 May

433	Spring birds	£112/138

Field Studies Council at Nettlecombe
Court *Taunton, Somerset*

1–4 May

434	Stained glass	£162

Higham Hall *Cockermouth*
ARCA

1–4 May

435	The fugitive king	£AFD

Univ Liverpool *Worcester*

1–6 May

436	Exploring west Somerset	£173/215

Field Studies Council at Nettlecombe
Court *Taunton, Somerset*

1–8 May

437	Spring birds of Snowdonia, Anglesey and the North Wales coast	£185/262

Field Studies Council at
Rhyd-y-creuau *Betws-y-coed*

1–8 May

438	Silk painting	£AFD

Wye Valley Arts Centre *St. Briavel's,*
Glos
ARCA

1–31 May

439	Bird watching	£45*
440	Flower arranging	£50*
441	Drawing, oil painting and watercolours	£40*
442	Basket making with cane	£50*
443	Rush seating	£45*
444	Cane seating	£45*
445	Needlecraft	£40*
446	Pottery (any Thursday)	£50
447	Rural surprises (any weekend: minimum of 6 people)	£175

1–31 May continued

448 Woodwork (any
consecutive 3 days
except Sunday) £165

449 Furniture restoration (any
consecutive 3 days
except Sunday) £165

450 Landscape painting (any
Sunday/Friday) £375

451 Chair making (any
Monday/Friday:
minimum of 2 people) £250

452 Bookbinding (any
Monday/Friday:
minimum of 2 people) £250

Acorn Activities *Herefordshire,
Shropshire and Wales*
**Per day. Bookings can be made for
any number of days.*

2–3 May

453 Woodturning £150

Acorn Activities *Herefordshire,
Shropshire and Wales*

2–5 May

454 Woodwind and brass
playing £214

HF Holidays *Whitby*

2–7 May

455 Batik and fabric painting £AFD

Wye Valley Arts Centre *St. Briavel's,
Glos*
ARCA

2–8 May

456 Geology of Arran £349

HF Holidays *Isle of Arran*

457 Woodwind and brass
playing £369

HF Holidays *Whitby*

3–6 May

458 Painting pastels in
springtime £110/150

Alston Hall Residential College
Preston
ARCA

3–8 May

459 Alexander Technique £284

460 T'ai Chi £269

HF Holidays *Dovedale*

3–8 May

461 Embroidery £229

Knuston Hall *Irchester*
ARCA

3–8 May

462 Woodturning £AFD

463 Drawing and painting
landscape £AFD

464 Landscape painting £AFD

West Dean College *Chichester*
ARCA

4–6 May

465 Marketing on the
Internet £92

Knuston Hall *Irchester*
ARCA

4–8 May

466 Spring nature
photography £167/220

**Field Studies Council at Juniper Hall
Field Centre** *Dorking*

4–8 May

467 English medieval
architecture £314

HF Holidays *Abingworth*

4–8 May

468 England's stout bastion £205

Higham Hall *Cockermouth*
ARCA

4–8 May

469 Porcelain restoration –
intermediate £245

**Mowbray School of Porcelain
Restoration** *Hatfield, Herts*

5–6 May

470 Life drawing £AFD

Barn Crafts *Fincham, Norfolk*
Accommodation arranged on request.

5–7 May

471 Summer birds of the Lee
Valley Park £90

Wansfell College *Theydon Bois*
ARCA

5–8 May

472 Bridge – overcalling £170/175

Hawthorn Bridge *Eastbourne, Sussex*

5–8 May

473	Birdwatching in the Brecon Beacons	£254

HF Holidays *Brecon*

5–8 May

474	Chinese brush painting	£127

Wansfell College *Theydon Bois*
ARCA

6–8 May

475	The countryside in spring	£75/100

Alston Hall Residential College
Preston
ARCA

6–8 May

476	Barber shop singing	£179

HF Holidays *Whitby*

6–8 May

477	WWW page design	£92

Knuston Hall *Irchester*
ARCA

6–8 May

478	Calligraphy for all	£82
479	Drama	£82

Lancashire College *Chorley*
ARCA

6–10 May

480	British sign language stage III – module III	£875

Lancashire College *Chorley*
ARCA

7–12 May

481	Norfolk: history and landscapes 1050–1650	£AFD

Univ Liverpool *Norwich*

8–9 May

482	Acrylics	£AFD

Barn Crafts *Fincham, Norfolk*
Accommodation arranged on request.

8–10 May

483	The city of Rome: art and power	£75/100
484	Assertiveness for women	£75/100
485	Viol and consort playing	£75/100

Alston Hall Residential College
Preston
ARCA

8–10 May

486	Book binding and repairs	£75/95
487	Marbling	£75/95

Belstead House *Ipswich*
ARCA

8–10 May

488	String chamber music	£122/142
489	Elementary keyboard	£91/111

Benslow Music Trust *Hitchin*
ARCA

8–10 May

490	Creative writing	£65

Carberry *Musselburgh, Edinburgh*

8–10 May

491	Spring gardens	£AFD
492	Photography	£AFD
493	Embroidery	£AFD

Dartington Hall *Totnes, Devon*

8–10 May

494	Monuments in the landscape	£105/120

Dillington House *Ilminster*
ARCA

8–10 May

495	Have a go at rock climbing	£96/120

Field Studies Council at Castle Head
Field Centre *Grange-over-Sands*

8–10 May

496	Bird songs and calls	£82/105
497	Microscopy for beekeepers	£82/105
498	Walking with a sketchbook	£82/105
499	Watercolour for absolute beginners	£82/105

Field Studies Council at Flatford Mill
Field Centre *East Bergholt*

8–10 May
500   Grass identification in
      spring   £78/102
**Field Studies Council at Juniper Hall
Field Centre** *Dorking*

8–10 May
501   Look out for mammals:
      an identification
      workshop   £50/90
**Field Studies Council at Nettlecombe
Court** *Taunton, Somerset*

8–10 May
502   Freshwater invertebrates £85/115
503   Wild flowers for pleasure £75/105
**Field Studies Council at Preston
Montford Field Centre** *Shrewsbury*

8–10 May
504   Flower arranging   £112
505   Wagner   £112
Higham Hall *Cockermouth*
ARCA

8–10 May
506   First steps to parchment
      craft   £92
507   Rags to riches   £92
508   Elementary recorders   £92
509   Acoustic guitar for
      beginners   £92
Knuston Hall *Irchester*
ARCA

8–10 May
510   French   £96
Lancashire College *Chorley*
ARCA

8–10 May
511   Antique glass   £99
512   More literary prize
      winners   £99
Maryland College *Woburn*
ARCA

8–10 May
513   Festival of Verdi   £AFD
514   The tao of clowning   £AFD
515   Plenty of plaits   £AFD
516   Still life painting –
      Cézanne   £AFD
517   Birds in your garden   £AFD
518   Landscape and gardens
      history   £AFD
519   Large format
      photography   £AFD
520   C & G embroidery –
      part I   £AFD
521   Home interior design –
      introduction   £AFD
Missenden Abbey *Great Missenden*
ARCA

8–10 May
522   Bridge – improvers   £AFD
523   An introduction to
      croquet   £AFD
524   Relax with raffia   £AFD
525   Flowers in watercolour   £AFD
The Old Rectory *Fittleworth*
ARCA

8–10 May
526   Choral weekend   £AFD
Summer Music *Henley on Thames*

8–10 May
527   A bird song weekend   £189
Univ Birmingham *Dumbleton, Worcs*

8–10 May
528   House detectives   £120
529   Spring birds   £120
530   Reading classical Greek:
      advanced   £120
531   The Proscenium Arch
      gives way to Theatre in
      the Round   £120
Univ Cambridge *Madingley Hall*

8–10 May
532   Birds for beginners   £AFD
Univ Nottingham *Gibraltar Point Field
Station*

8–10 May
533   Geology for walkers   £AFD
534   Tai Chi and meditation   £AFD
Urchfont Manor College *Devizes*
ARCA

8–10 May
535 Churchill: a study in
leadership £85
Wansfell College *Theydon Bois*
ARCA

8–10 May
536 Cavaliers and
Roundheads £70
Wedgwood Memorial College
Barlaston
ARCA

8–10 May
537 Singers workshop £84
538 Ancient Egyptian
painting £84
Wensum Lodge *Norwich*
ARCA

8–10 May
539 Woodturning £AFD
West Dean College *Chichester*
ARCA

8–10 May
540 Plaster sculpture £AFD
541 Embroidery £AFD
Wye Valley Arts Centre *St. Briavel's,*
Glos
ARCA

8–13 May
542 Landscape painting £255
Painting in Pembrokeshire *St. David's*

9–10 May
543 Pottery £100
Acorn Activities *Herefordshire,*
Shropshire and Wales

9–10 May
544 Introduction to insect
identification and
ecology £38
Field Studies Council at Epping Forest
Field Centre *Loughton, Essex*

9–10 May
Misbourne Weekend
545 Upholstery restoration £AFD
546 Batik workshop £AFD
547 Wet into wet
watercolour £AFD
548 Picture framing £AFD
549 Clay sculpture – find your
medium £AFD
550 Success with stained
glass £AFD
551 Life drawing and painting £AFD
552 Silversmithing £AFD
553 The art of mosaics £AFD
554 C & G woodcarving £AFD
555 Fine art painting –
BOCN: painting the
spring landscape £AFD
Missenden Abbey *Great Missenden*
ARCA

9–10 May
556 Tarot: diploma part I £60
Mountain Hall *Queensbury*
Price includes tuition/lunches.
Accommodation/dinner, B/B £25 per
night.

9–15 May
557 Scrabble, walking and
sightseeing
(experienced) £374
HF Holidays *Brecon*
558 Birdwatching in
Snowdonia and the
Conwy estuary £349
HF Holidays *Conwy*

10–15 May
559 Chinese brush painting £260
Higham Hall *Cockermouth*
ARCA

10–15 May
560 Insights – social and
cultural studies for
visually impaired £140
Wedgwood Memorial College
Barlaston
ARCA

10–15 May

561	Spring flower painting	£AFD
562	Gilding part I	£AFD
563	Painting – variations on a theme	£AFD
564	Silk painting workshop II	£AFD

West Dean College *Chichester*
ARCA

10–15 May

565	Flowers in watercolour	£AFD

Wye Valley Arts Centre *St. Briavel's, Glos*
ARCA

10–16 May

566	Watercolour week	£169/397

Weobley Art Centre *Weobley, Herefordshire*
ARCA

11–13 May

567	The Celestine Prophecy	£82

Lancashire College *Chorley*
ARCA

11–13 May

568	The American Civil War	£85
569	Copper and pewterwork	£85

Wansfell College *Theydon Bois*
ARCA

11–14 May

570	Victorian centres: The Westminster Review at mid-century	£65*

Birkbeck College Univ London *London*
**non-residential.*

11–14 May

571	Art appreciation	£147

Burton Manor College *South Wirral*
ARCA

11–14 May

572	Certificate in the theory of counselling	£139

Lancashire College *Chorley*
ARCA

11–15 May

573	Simply flowers	£140/200

Field Studies Council at Preston
Montford Field Centre *Shrewsbury*

11–15 May

574	Porcelain restoration – advanced	£255

Mowbray School of Porcelain Restoration *Hatfield, Herts*

11–15 May

575	Rudyard Kipling – his life and works	£AFD
576	Landscape in watercolour	£AFD
577	Traditional miniature painting	£AFD

The Old Rectory *Fittleworth*
ARCA

11–15 May

578	Special needs in the countryside	£380

Scottish Field Studies Association *Kindrogan Field Centre Pitlochry*

12–13 May

579	Sculpture	£AFD

Barn Crafts *Fincham, Norfolk*
Accommodation arranged on request.

12–14 May

580	Child psychology	£82

Lancashire College *Chorley*
ARCA

12–14 May

581	Recorder playing	£AFD
582	Découpage	£AFD

Pendrell Hall College *Staffs*
ARCA

13–15 May

583	Landscape photography	£164

HF Holidays *Derwentwater*

13–15 May

584	Introduction to mosaic	£82

Lancashire College *Chorley*
ARCA

15–16 May

585	Watercolour painting on location	£AFD

Barn Crafts *Fincham, Norfolk*
Accommodation arranged on request.

15–17 May
586 Wildlife weekend –
Montgomeryshire £150
Acorn Activities *Herefordshire,*
Shropshire and Wales

15–17 May
587 Chinese brush painting –
beginners £75/100
588 Embroidery: icons and
angels £75/100
Alston Hall Residential College
Preston
ARCA

15–17 May
589 Christ, stress and glory
(Christ centred
management of stress) £AFD
590 The Holocaust in
literature £69
Ammerdown Centre *Radstock, Bath*

15–17 May
591 Foundation course for
strings £87/107
592 Further theory £95/115
Benslow Music Trust *Hitchin*
ARCA

15–17 May
593 Astronomy from square
one £98
Burton Manor College *South Wirral*
ARCA

15–17 May
594 Taoism £AFD
595 Delight in books £AFD
Dartington Hall *Totnes, Devon*

15–17 May
596 Spring flowers in south
Lakeland £80/104
Field Studies Council at Castle Head
Field Centre *Grange-over-Sands*

15–17 May
597 Photography – working
with close-up and flash £82/105
598 Family birdwatching £AFD
599 Improve your
watercolours £82/105
600 National Trust properties
in Suffolk: behind the
scenes £82/105
601 Painting and drawing for
families £AFD
Field Studies Council at Flatford Mill
Field Centre *East Bergholt*

15–17 May
602 Working with
watercolours £78/102
Field Studies Council at Juniper Hall
Field Centre *Dorking*

15–17 May
603 A naturalist in Shropshire £75/105
604 Landscape painting in
watercolour £75/105
Field Studies Council at Preston
Montford Field Centre *Shrewsbury*

15–17 May
605 Flower painting £112
606 George Gershwin
centenary course £112
Higham Hall *Cockermouth*
ARCA

15–17 May
607 Metal thread embroidery £88
608 Welsh weekend £88
609 In quest of King Arthur £98
610 Wagner £88
611 Flowers in watercolour £88
The Hill Residential Centre
Abergavenny
ARCA

15–17 May
612 Ancient Middle East
society £AFD
613 Creative lacemaking £86
Horncastle College *Horncastle*
ARCA

15–17 May

614	Patchwork and quilting	£92
615	Lichens	£92
616	Drawing for watercolours	£92
617	Computing with Windows '95	£92

Knuston Hall *Irchester*
ARCA

15–17 May

618	Greek	£96
619	Writing autobiography	£96
620	Dutch	£96

Lancashire College *Chorley*
ARCA

15–17 May

621	Flowers and birds of early spring	£99
622	Divided visions: Britain and Ireland 1798–1922	£99

Maryland College *Woburn*
ARCA

15–17 May

623	Towards the millennium – history of the arts 1950/60	£AFD
624	Honiton lace	£AFD
625	Exploring acrylics	£AFD
626	Completing your tax return	£AFD
627	Writing romantic fiction	£AFD
628	French conversation – advanced	£AFD
629	C & G embroidery – part II	£AFD

Missenden Abbey *Great Missenden*
ARCA

15–17 May

630	Fabric painting for fun	£AFD
631	Introduction to desktop publishing	£AFD
632	Landscape and gardens in oils or acrylics	£AFD
633	Clarinet and flute weekend	£AFD

The Old Rectory *Fittleworth*
ARCA

15–17 May

634	Follow on watercolours	£AFD
635	Advanced bridge	£AFD
636	Machine knitting	£AFD

Pendrell Hall College *Staffs*
ARCA

15–17 May

637	Prehistoric Cotswolds: tombs, stones and circles	£221

Univ Birmingham *Dumbleton, Worcs*

15–17 May

638	Geology of the area between Matlock and Buxton	£AFD

Univ Liverpool *Matlock*

15–17 May

639	Medieval Lincoln	£AFD

Univ Nottingham *Lincoln*

640	The lyric from courtly love to Cole Porter	£AFD

Univ Nottingham *London*

15–17 May

641	Painters and places	£AFD
642	Audiovisual presentations	£AFD

Urchfont Manor College *Devizes*
ARCA

15–17 May

643	Egypt: King Akhenaten	£85
644	*Tosca* and *Jenufa*	£85

Wansfell College *Theydon Bois*
ARCA

15–17 May

645	Europe 2000 – 10th Annual Raymond Williams Weekend	£67

Wedgwood Memorial College
Barlaston
ARCA

15–17 May
646 Calligraphy – letterform –
    Gothic for today   £AFD
647 Surface finishes for
    decorative paintwork   £AFD
648 Imagination through
    painting   £AFD
649 Creative drawing
    workshop   £AFD
650 Practical work – planning
    for silversmithing
    projects   £AFD
651 Simple print techniques
    for textiles   £AFD
West Dean College *Chichester*
ARCA

15–17 May
652 Hand coloured
    photographs   £AFD
653 Beginner's drawing and
    monoprinting   £AFD
Wye Valley Arts Centre *St. Briavel's,*
Glos
ARCA

15–18 May
654 Silversmithing   £115/160
Alston Hall Residential College
Preston
ARCA

15–18 May
655 Stained glass   £AFD
West Dean College *Chichester*
ARCA

16–17 May
656 Bridge for beginners   £80
657 Gourmet cooking   £120
658 Garden design   £100
659 Watercolour for the
    terrified   £96
660 Stained glass   £120
Acorn Activities *Herefordshire,*
Shropshire and Wales

16–17 May
661 Forest spiders   £32
Field Studies Council at Epping Forest
Field Centre *Loughton, Essex*

16–17 May
662 Hypnotism/self-hypnosis   £60
Mountain Hall *Queensbury*
Price includes tuition/lunches.
Accommodation/dinner, B/B £25 per
night.

16–17 May
663 The Peak District   £AFD
Univ Manchester *Manchester*

16–22 May
664 Birdwatching in
    Northumberland and the
    Farnes   £369
HF Holidays *Alnmouth*
665 Birdwatching in Arran   £379
HF Holidays *Isle of Arran*
666 Spring in Sussex   £429
HF Holidays *Abingworth*
667 Historic Wight   £359
HF Holidays *Isle of Wight*
668 Drawing and walking   £369
HF Holidays *Derwentwater*
669 Landscape photography   £386
HF Holidays *Coniston Water*
670 Historic railways in the
    rural Midlands   £449
HF Holidays *Dovedale*
671 Play your electronic
    keyboard – intermediates   £334
HF Holidays *Freshwater Bay*

17–19 May
672 Garden and plant
    photography   £AFD
West Dean College *Chichester*
ARCA

17–20 May
673 Silversmithing   £AFD
674 Painting – exploring the
    imagination   £AFD
West Dean College *Chichester*
ARCA

17–22 May
675 Abstracts in pastels   £260
676 Fly fishing in Lakeland   £260
Higham Hall *Cockermouth*
ARCA

17–22 May
677 Cabinet making – part 2 £AFD
678 Painting gardens in
    watercolour £AFD
West Dean College *Chichester*
ARCA

17–22 May
679 Drawing explored £AFD
Wye Valley Arts Centre *St. Briavel's,*
Glos
ARCA

17–24 May
680 Creative writing £AFD
Wye Valley Arts Centre *St. Briavel's,*
Glos
ARCA

18–20 May
681 Gardens of the North
    West £82
Lancashire College *Chorley*
ARCA

18–20 May
682 Come into the garden £95
Wansfell College *Theydon Bois*
ARCA

18–21 May
683 Group quartet workshop £110/135
Benslow Music Trust *Hitchin*
ARCA

18–21 May
684 Italia 2000 £139
Lancashire College *Chorley*
ARCA

18–22 May
685 Composers of Sussex £AFD
686 Sculpture – carving and
    modelling £AFD
687 Ink, line and watercolour £AFD
The Old Rectory *Fittleworth*
ARCA

19–20 May
688 Embroidery without kits £AFD
Barn Crafts *Fincham, Norfolk*
Accommodation arranged on request.

19–21 May
689 China painting £AFD
Pendrell Hall College *Staffs*
ARCA

20–24 May
690 Chinese brush painting £AFD
Hawkwood College *Stroud, Glos*
ARCA

22–23 May
691 Interior design on a
    budget £AFD
Barn Crafts *Fincham, Norfolk*
Accommodation arranged on request.

22–24 May
692 Marine and coastal
    landscapes £75/95
Belstead House *Ipswich*
ARCA

22–24 May
693 Improve your
    watercolours £82/105
694 Spring birdwatching £82/105
695 Trees and tree
    identification in spring £82/105
696 Walking in Constable
    Country £82/105
Field Studies Council at Flatford Mill
Field Centre *East Bergholt*

22–24 May
697 Spring walking £78/102
698 Woodland leaf-litter
    invertebrates £78/102
Field Studies Council at Juniper Hall
Field Centre *Dorking*

22–24 May
699 Birdwatching in the
    Yorkshire Dales £80/105
700 Nature and landscape
    photography in the
    Yorkshire Dales £85/110
Field Studies Council at Malham Tarn
Field Centre *Settle, N Yorks*

22–24 May
701 Painting the landscape £75/105
Field Studies Council at Preston
Montford Field Centre *Shrewsbury*

22–24 May

| 702 | Spring flowers of South Devon | £79/105 |

Field Studies Council at Slapton Ley
Field Centre *Kingsbridge, Devon*

22–24 May

703	Goldsmithing	£88
704	Creative embroidery	£88
705	Writers workshop	£88

The Hill Residential Centre
Abergavenny
ARCA

22–24 May

| 706 | 3D Découpage | £86 |

Horncastle College *Horncastle*
ARCA

22–24 May

707	An invitation to croquet	£92
708	Alexander Technique	£118
709	Wine tasting	£122
710	A law unto ourselves	£AFD

Knuston Hall *Irchester*
ARCA

22–24 May

| 711 | Painting in watercolour and oil | £99 |
| 712 | French conversation – intermediate level | £99 |

Maryland College *Woburn*
ARCA

22–24 May

713	Sketching and walking	£AFD
714	Visiting the Sussex past	£AFD
715	Croquet encore	£AFD
716	Write your own autobiography	£AFD

The Old Rectory *Fittleworth*
ARCA

22–24 May

717	Wildflowers	£91
718	Bird sounds	£91
719	Spring walking	£89
720	Family/children's courses	£57*

Scottish Field Studies Association
Kindrogan Field Centre Pitlochry
*Children and discounts.

22–24 May

721	Iris Murdoch: philosophy, religion and the novel	£120
722	Devices and desires: Shakespearean comedy	£120
723	Russian weekend	£120
724	Islamic architecture	£120

Univ Cambridge *Madingley Hall*

22–24 May

| 725 | Roman art and architecture | ·£AFD |
| 726 | Wood engraving | £AFD |

Urchfont Manor College *Devizes*
ARCA

22–24 May

727	Villages of East London	£95
728	Forbidden questions	£85
729	Art and propaganda: the patronage of the Dukes of Burgundy 1364–1477	£85

Wansfell College *Theydon Bois*
ARCA

22–24 May

| 730 | Weaving with words – creative poetry | £70 |

Wedgwood Memorial College
Barlaston
ARCA

22–24 May

731	Parish churches of Norwich	£84
732	Mah Jong	£84
733	Colour analysis and style	£84

Wensum Lodge *Norwich*
ARCA

22–24 May

| 734 | Life drawing | £AFD |

West Dean College *Chichester*
ARCA

22–25 May

| 735 | Recording techniques | £105/130 |
| 736 | Musicals and operetta | £105/130 |

Benslow Music Trust *Hitchin*
ARCA

22–25 May
737   Darganfod Sir Benfro ar
       droed (Cwrs Cymraeg)   £142
Field Studies Council at Dale Fort
Field Centre *Haverfordwest*

22–25 May
738   Family naturalist and bird
       weekend   £AFD
739   Introduction to DMap
       and recorder   £100/135
740   Origins of Darwin: his
       early life in Shropshire £100/135
Field Studies Council at Preston
Montford Field Centre *Shrewsbury*

22–25 May
741   Bridge – modernise your
       acol bidding   £180
Hawthorn Bridge *Honiley, nr Warwick*

22–25 May
742   Spring bridge   £162
743   Bags of quilting   £162
Higham Hall *Cockermouth*
ARCA

22–25 May
744   Gardens around Warwick   £AFD
Univ Nottingham *Royal Leamington
Spa*
745   The Malvern Music
       Festival   £AFD
Univ Nottingham *Malvern*

22–25 May
746   Printmaking workshop   £AFD
747   Framing workshop   £AFD
748   Painting bluebell woods
       and the landscape   £AFD
749   Cane and rush seating,
       willow basketry   £AFD
750   Waistcoats and exotic
       accessories   £AFD
West Dean College *Chichester*
ARCA

22–26 May
751   Painting in your favourite
       medium   £150/200
752   Calligraphy   £150/200
753   Stained glass workshop £150/200
Alston Hall Residential College
Preston
ARCA

22–26 May
754   Birds: sight and sound in
       early summer   £90/148
Field Studies Council at Preston
Montford Field Centre *Shrewsbury*

22–27 May
755   Photography   £AFD
West Dean College *Chichester*
ARCA

22–29 May
756   Stained glass and glass
       painting   £221/280
Field Studies Council at Flatford Mill
Field Centre *East Bergholt*

22–29 May
757   Birdwatching in the
       Yorkshire Dales   £200/270
758   Mosses and liverworts   £200/270
759   Nature and landscape
       photography in the
       Yorkshire Dales   £205/275
Field Studies Council at Malham Tarn
Field Centre *Settle, N Yorks*

22–29 May
760   Woodland plants   £209/268
Field Studies Council at Nettlecombe
Court *Taunton, Somerset*

22–29 May
761   Spring nature
       photography   £195/270
Field Studies Council at Preston
Montford Field Centre *Shrewsbury*

23–24 May
762   Aromatherapy/massage   £60
Mountain Hall *Queensbury*
*Price includes tuition/lunches.
Accommodation/dinner, B/B £25 per
night.*

23–30 May
763   Spring birds of the coast,
       woods and valleys   £209/268
Field Studies Council at Dale Fort
Field Centre *Haverfordwest*

23–30 May
764   Birdwatching in South
       Devon   £369
HF Holidays *Thurlestone Sands*

23–30 May
765   Geology of Islay   £AFD
Univ Liverpool *Islay, Scotland*

24–29 May
766   Butterflies and moths   £190/240
Field Studies Council at Castle Head
Field Centre *Grange-over-Sands*

24–29 May
767   Painting plants: late
        spring colours   £168/215
Field Studies Council at Flatford Mill
Field Centre *East Bergholt*

24–29 May
768   Introduction to lichens   £201/256
Field Studies Council at
Rhyd-y-creuau *Betws-y-coed*

24–29 May
769   Pottery general –
        handbuilding and
        throwing   £AFD
West Dean College *Chichester*
ARCA

24–29 May
770   Watercolour painting   £AFD
Wye Valley Arts Centre *St. Briavel's,
Glos*
ARCA

24–30 May
771   Pottery with other
        activities   £395
Acorn Activities *Herefordshire,
Shropshire and Wales*

24–30 May
772   Watercolour week   £169/397
Weobley Art Centre *Weobley,
Herefordshire*
ARCA

25–28 May
773   Contemporary rag rugs
        and wallhangings   £125
774   Brush up your bridge   £105/120
775   Painting – how to start
        and progress   £105/120
Dillington House *Ilminster*
ARCA

25–29 May
776   Biological recording
        techniques   £175/225
Field Studies Council at Preston
Montford Field Centre *Shrewsbury*

25–29 May
777   Spring wild flowers of
        Snowdonia and the
        North Wales Coast   £135/179
Field Studies Council at
Rhyd-y-creuau *Betws-y-coed*

25–29 May
778   Mozart's operas   £205
779   The Lever Art Gallery   £225
Higham Hall *Cockermouth*
ARCA

25–29 May
780   Bookbinding and book
        restoration   £AFD
Urchfont Manor College *Devizes*
ARCA

25–31 May
781   Country chairmaking   £AFD
West Dean College *Chichester*
ARCA

26–27 May
782   Enamelling pictures   £AFD
Barn Crafts *Fincham, Norfolk*
Accommodation arranged on request.

26–28 May
783   Elementary recorder
        ensemble   £91/111
Benslow Music Trust *Hitchin*
ARCA

26–28 May
784   Practical lacemaking   £94
Horncastle College *Horncastle*
ARCA

26–29 May
785   Discover the beauty of
        watercolours   £150/200
Alston Hall Residential College
Preston
ARCA

26–29 May
786 Benchmarks in wine £120/150
Belstead House *Ipswich*
ARCA

26–29 May
787 Discovering Lincolnshire
– towns and villages £AFD
Univ Nottingham *Horncastle College*
Lincs

26–29 May
788 Practical painting:
acrylics £127
Wansfell College *Theydon Bois*
ARCA

27–29 May
789 Modern sound recording £82
790 Make the most of your
camcorder £82
791 Introduction to modern
jazz £82
Lancashire College *Chorley*
ARCA

27–29 May
792 Wildlife of Essex nature
reserves £90
793 Georgian London:
Kensington Palace to
Carlton House £95
Wansfell College *Theydon Bois*
ARCA

27–29 May
794 Propagation for your own
garden £AFD
West Dean College *Chichester*
ARCA

29–30 May
795 Life drawing £AFD
Barn Crafts *Fincham, Norfolk*
Accommodation arranged on request.

29–31 May
796 Elgar birthday weekend £175
Acorn Activities *Herefordshire,*
Shropshire and Wales

29–31 May
797 Tai Chi weekend £75/100
798 Bobbin lacemaking £75/100
Alston Hall Residential College
Preston
ARCA

29–31 May
799 Christian Arts
Conference – The
innocent eye – the
influence of Paul Klee £69
Ammerdown Centre *Radstock, Bath*

29–31 May
800 Wind ensembles £AFD
Belstead House *Ipswich*
ARCA

29–31 May
801 Viol consorts £97/117
802 Calling all workers £95/115
Benslow Music Trust *Hitchin*
ARCA

29–31 May
803 Britain's Romantic Age
(1780–1830) £85/110
804 Pictures from fabric £85/110
805 Photographing people
and architecture in
monochrome £85/110
806 An invitation to croquet £90/115
Dillington House *Ilminster*
ARCA

29–31 May
807 Lakeland farmland: an
ecological resource? £80/104
Field Studies Council at Castle Head
Field Centre *Grange-over-Sands*

29–31 May
808 Designing a garden for
wildlife £78/102
Field Studies Council at Juniper Hall
Field Centre *Dorking*

29–31 May

809	Bat ecology	£80/105
810	Rambling through the Yorkshire Dales	£80/105
811	Yorkshire gardens	£80/105
812	Look out for mammals – identification workshop	£50/90

Field Studies Council at Malham Tarn Field Centre *Settle, N Yorks*

29–31 May

813	Bat identification	£75/105
814	Biological recording with BIOBASE	£75/115
815	Housman's Shropshire	£75/105
816	Newts	£75/105

Field Studies Council at Preston Montford Field Centre *Shrewsbury*

29–31 May

817	Cartoon drawing	£112
818	Megaliths of the South West	£112
819	Paper making	£112

Higham Hall *Cockermouth*
ARCA

29–31 May

820	Mixed media	£88
821	Photography	£88
822	Quilting	£88
823	Intermediate bridge	£88

The Hill Residential Centre *Abergavenny*
ARCA

29–31 May

824	Whitework embroidery	£86
825	Glasscraft	£86
826	Sketching and painting	£86

Horncastle College *Horncastle*
ARCA

29–31 May

827	Stained glass	£96
828	Garlands, garlands all the way	£96
829	Alexander Technique	£96
830	Accelerated learning	£96

Lancashire College *Chorley*
ARCA

29–31 May

| 831 | Furniture: Hepplewhite and Sheraton | £99 |
| 832 | Taking the waters: spas and seaside resorts 1550–1950 | £99 |

Maryland College *Woburn*
ARCA

29–31 May

833	Tai Ji Quan and Chinese health arts	£AFD
834	How to write/illustrate picture books for children	£AFD
835	Drawing for the terrified	£AFD
836	Art decoded – C19th	£AFD
837	The Gallipoli campaign revisited	£AFD
838	Relating to yourself and others	£AFD
839	Improving your memory	£AFD
840	Tasting tea and coffee	£AFD
841	Machine embroidery BOCN	£AFD

Missenden Abbey *Great Missenden*
ARCA

29–31 May

842	Chinese brush painting	£AFD
843	Stress counselling/ management	£AFD
844	Beaded amulet purses	£AFD

Pendrell Hall College *Staffs*
ARCA

29–31 May

845	Spring birds	£91
846	Introducing mosses	£91
847	Natural history of the Highlands	£89

Scottish Field Studies Association *Kindrogan Field Centre Pitlochry*

29–31 May

848	Towns in East Anglia: the early years	£120
849	Monitoring for wildlife conservation	£120
850	The First World War: the naval dimension	£120
851	Humanities computing – introduction	£120

Univ Cambridge *Madingley Hall*

29–31 May
852 The story of Australia £AFD
853 The X-files £AFD
Univ Nottingham *Horncastle College Lincs*

29–31 May
854 Painting spring flowers £AFD
855 Egyptology £AFD
Urchfont Manor College *Devizes*
ARCA

29–31 May
856 Bridge: every hand
counts £85
857 Tai Chi Ch'Uan £85
858 The willow pattern £95
Wansfell College *Theydon Bois*
ARCA

29–31 May
859 A pianist's journey
through the C19th £70
860 Lewis Carroll – logician,
photographer and
Wonderland £70
Wedgwood Memorial College
Barlaston
ARCA

29–31 May
861 Textured embroidery £AFD
862 Colour and expression in
landscape painting £AFD
863 Sketchbook to finished
painting £AFD
864 Full creative control of
your SLR camera £AFD
West Dean College *Chichester*
ARCA

29–31 May
865 Stained glass study £AFD
866 Feng Shui – colour for
the home £AFD
Wye Valley Arts Centre *St. Briavel's,*
Glos
ARCA

29 May–1 June
867 Lakeland in spring £112/148
868 Mosses, liverworts and
lichens £112/148
Field Studies Council at Blencathra
Field Centre *Threlkeld, Keswick*

29 May–1 June
869 Photography – working
with colour £110/140
870 Garden flowers and
garden design £110/140
871 Watercolour for absolute
beginners £110/140
Field Studies Council at Flatford Mill
Field Centre *East Bergholt*

29 May–1 June
872 Mosaics in marble, glass
and stone £AFD
West Dean College *Chichester*
ARCA

29 May–5 June
873 Photographing Lakeland
in spring £205/268
874 Watercolour painting £205/268
Field Studies Council at Blencathra
Field Centre *Threlkeld, Keswick*

29 May–5 June
875 Dolls house summer
school £AFD
876 Fittleworth singers
summer school £AFD
877 The wildlife of Sussex £AFD
The Old Rectory *Fittleworth*
ARCA

30–31 May
878 Silversmithing and
jewellery £120
Acorn Activities *Herefordshire,*
Shropshire and Wales

30 May–5 June
879 Birdwatching in
Perthshire £414
HF Holidays *Pitlochry*
880 Birdwatching in the
Highlands £369
HF Holidays *Loch Leven*
881 Wildlife of the Lakes £389
HF Holidays *Coniston Water*
882 Landscape photography £409
HF Holidays *Bourton-on-the-Water*
883 Castles of North Wales £429
HF Holidays *Conwy*

54

31 May–5 June
884 Landscape painting £385
Painting in Pembrokeshire *St. David's*

31 May–5 June
885 The basics of
    watercolour landscape £AFD
886 Lettering on handmade
    books £AFD
887 Sculptural modelling for
    plant containers £AFD
West Dean College *Chichester*
ARCA

31 May–5 June
888 Landscape for beginners £AFD
Wye Valley Arts Centre *St. Briavel's, Glos*
ARCA

31 May–6 June
889 Back on track
    (watercolour tuition for
    the self-taught) £169/397
Weobley Art Centre *Weobley, Herefordshire*
ARCA

■   ■   ■   ■

June 1998

☐   ☐   ☐   ☐

1–3 June
890 Scented plants and
    gardens £AFD
West Dean College *Chichester*
ARCA

1–4 June
891 Family history £127
Wansfell College *Theydon Bois*
ARCA

1–4 June
892 Gardens ponds and
    water features £AFD
West Dean College *Chichester*
ARCA

1–5 June
893 Crafts summer school £82
Lancashire College *Chorley*
ARCA

1–5 June
894 Porcelain restoration –
    beginners £235
**Mowbray School of Porcelain
Restoration** *Hatfield, Herts*

1–5 June
895 Summer school: German
    language through
    literature *Buddenbrooks* £170
Wansfell College *Theydon Bois*
ARCA

1–5 June
896 Not all landscapes are
    green – colour in
    landscape painting £136
Wedgwood Memorial College
Barlaston
ARCA

1–30 June
897 Bird watching £45*
898 Flower arranging £50*
899 Drawing, oil painting and
    watercolours £40*
900 Basket making with cane £50*
901 Rush seating £45*
902 Cane seating £45*
903 Needlecraft £40*
904 Pottery (any Thursday) £50
905 Rural surprises (any
    weekend: minimum of 6
    people) £175

1–30 June continued

906	Woodwork (any consecutive 3 days except Sunday)	£165
907	Furniture restoration (any consecutive 3 days except Sunday)	£165
908	Landscape painting (any Sunday/Friday)	£375
909	Chair making (any Monday/Friday: minimum of 2 people)	£250
910	Bookbinding (any Monday/Friday: minimum of 2 people)	£250

Acorn Activities *Herefordshire, Shropshire and Wales*
* Per day. Bookings can be made for any number of days.

2–3 June

911	Sculpture	£AFD

Barn Crafts *Fincham, Norfolk*
Accommodation arranged on request.

2–5 June

912	Visitor safety	£304

Scottish Field Studies Association
Kindrogan Field Centre Pitlochry

3–6 June

913	An introduction to SLR photography	£111/142

Field Studies Council at Dale Fort
Field Centre *Haverfordwest*

4–8 June

914	Diving the Skomer Marine Reserve and Pembrokeshire Islands	£160/205

Field Studies Council at Dale Fort
Field Centre *Haverfordwest*

5–6 June

915	Watercolour painting on location	£AFD

Barn Crafts *Fincham, Norfolk*
Accommodation arranged on request.

5–7 June

916	Wildlife weekend – Pembrokeshire	£150

Acorn Activities *Herefordshire, Shropshire and Wales*

5–7 June

917	Ruskin lacemaking	£75/100
918	Writing short stories	£75/100

Alston Hall Residential College
Preston
ARCA

5–7 June

919	Playford dance	£75/95

Belstead House *Ipswich*
ARCA

5–7 June

920	Wind chamber music	£91/111

Benslow Music Trust *Hitchin*
ARCA

5–7 June

921	The shaping of C16th Spain	£79/105
922	The formation of Christendom	£90/115

Dillington House *Ilminster*
ARCA

5–7 June

923	Spring flowers in the Lake District	£90/114
924	Steam weekend	£100/124

Field Studies Council at Blencathra
Field Centre *Threlkeld, Keswick*

5–7 June

925	Container gardening	£82/105
926	Painting plants in garden settings	£82/105
927	Walking John Constable's landscapes	£82/105
928	Watercolour for near beginners	£82/105

Field Studies Council at Flatford Mill
Field Centre *East Bergholt*

5–7 June

929	Orchids	£81/102
930	Photographing wild flowers	£88/112
931	Tatting	£78/102

Field Studies Council at Juniper Hall
Field Centre *Dorking*

5–7 June

932	Art appreciation	£AFD

Higham Hall *Cockermouth*
ARCA

5–7 June

933	Mah Jong	£92
934	Special clothes	£92

Knuston Hall *Irchester*
ARCA

5–7 June

935	Spanish	£96
936	Counselling skills II	£96

Lancashire College *Chorley*
ARCA

5–7 June

937	American line dancing	£99
938	Quilting	£99

Maryland College *Woburn*
ARCA

5–7 June

939	Jazz – an introduction	£AFD
940	Modern painting series: expressionism	£AFD
941	Successful watercolour	£AFD
942	UFOs – embroidery surgery	£AFD
943	Poetry and prose of the Thirties	£AFD
944	Gardens in watercolour	£AFD
945	Meditation to quieten the mind	£AFD
946	Colour prints from slides	£AFD
947	Bead needle weaving BOCN	£AFD

Missenden Abbey *Great Missenden*
ARCA

5–7 June

948	Stockmarket and investment for beginners	£AFD
949	Painting: wet in wet	£AFD
950	Making a traditional collectors teddy bear	£AFD

The Old Rectory *Fittleworth*
ARCA

5–7 June

951	Old English cottages	£AFD
952	Getting to know your PC	£AFD
953	Jewellery and silver making	£AFD

Pendrell Hall College *Staffs*
ARCA

5–7 June

954	Guitar ensembles	£AFD
955	Putting over a song	£AFD

Summer Music *Hassocks, Sussex*

5–7 June

956	Birds around the Long Mynd	£170

Univ Birmingham *Church Stretton, Shropshire*

5–7 June

957	Extinctions: crises in the history of life	£120
958	Botanical illustration	£120
959	French weekend	£120
960	Shakespeare and Rome	£120

Univ Cambridge *Madingley Hall*

5–7 June

961	Bats in the belfry	£AFD

Univ Nottingham *Gibraltar Point Field Station*

962	Victorian and Edwardian theatres	£AFD

Univ Nottingham *Sheffield*

5–7 June

963	Aristotle	£AFD

Urchfont Manor College *Devizes*
ARCA

5–7 June

964	Wildlife of woodlands, wetlands	£85
965	Anthony Trollope: character and morality in *Phineas Finn* (1869) and *The Eustace Diamonds* (1873)	£85

Wansfell College *Theydon Bois*
ARCA

5–7 June

966	Conservation gardening	£70
967	Natural history photography	£70

Wedgwood Memorial College *Barlaston*
ARCA

5–7 June

968	Happy go lucky English	£84
969	Hand marbled papers	£84
970	Why worry – managing stress	£84

Wensum Lodge *Norwich*
ARCA

5–7 June

971	Basic blacksmithing	£AFD
972	Painting miniatures and silhouettes	£AFD
973	The basics of pure watercolour	£AFD
974	Cabinet making – part 1	£AFD
975	Caring for furniture	£AFD
976	Jewellery – rings with stone setting	£AFD
977	Glass engraving	£AFD

West Dean College *Chichester*
ARCA

5–8 June

978	Painting landscapes in watercolours	£111/142

Field Studies Council at Dale Fort
Field Centre *Haverfordwest*

5–12 June

979	In Wainwright's footsteps	£261/285

Field Studies Council at Blencathra
Field Centre *Threlkeld, Keswick*

5–12 June

980	Abstract painting	£AFD

Higham Hall *Cockermouth*
ARCA

5–12 June

981	Drawing and painting in all media	£AFD

Wye Valley Arts Centre *St. Briavel's,*
Glos
ARCA

6–7 June

982	Decorative interiors and paint effects	£100

Acorn Activities *Herefordshire,*
Shropshire and Wales

6–7 June

983	Ecological survey techniques	£38

Field Studies Council at Epping Forest
Field Centre *Loughton, Essex*

6–7 June

984	Rambling	£62
985	Hypnosis and relaxation – advanced	£AFD

Knuston Hall *Irchester*
ARCA

6–7 June
Misbourne Weekend

986	Porcelain restoration	£AFD
987	Upholstery restoration	£AFD
988	Drama series – directing	£AFD
989	Pottery – raku	£AFD
990	Glass painting	£AFD
991	Make and play an African drum	£AFD
992	Paper making, collage and papier maché workshop	£AFD
993	Jewellery BOCN	£AFD
994	Relief printmaking BOCN: multi-colour lino-cut, wood-cut and collograph	£AFD
995	Making new fabrics BOCN	£AFD

Missenden Abbey *Great Missenden*
ARCA

6–9 June

996	Nature photography in Pembrokeshire	£111/142

Field Studies Council at Dale Fort
Field Centre *Haverfordwest*

6–12 June

997	Theatre appreciation	£439

HF Holidays *Pitlochry*

998	Myths and legends of Northumbria	£409

HF Holidays *Alnmouth*

999	Antiques and great houses	£449

HF Holidays *Sedburgh*

1000	Historic houses of Lakeland	£409

HF Holidays *Coniston Water*

6–12 June continued
1001 Great little trains of
        Wales   £454
HF Holidays *Conwy*
1002 Great Scottish
        waterways   £389
HF Holidays *Loch Leven*

7–11 June
1003 Raku ceramics – a fresh
        approach   £AFD
West Dean College *Chichester*
ARCA

7–12 June
1004 Landscape painting   £385
Painting in Pembrokeshire *St. David's*

7–12 June
1005 Summer watercolours
        for improvers   £AFD
1006 Stone carving workshop   £AFD
1007 Creative blacksmithing   £AFD
West Dean College *Chichester*
ARCA

7–13 June
1008 Painting castles in
        watercolour   £169/397
Weobley Art Centre *Weobley,*
Herefordshire
ARCA

8–10 June
1009 Antiques appreciation   £82
Lancashire College *Chorley*
ARCA

8–11 June
1010 Jane Austen and the
        literature of her day   £65*
Birkbeck College Univ London
London
non-residential.

8–11 June
1011 The evolution of the
        British landscape   £137
Wansfell College *Theydon Bois*
ARCA

8–12 June
1012 Porcelain restoration –
        intermediate   £245
Mowbray School of Porcelain
Restoration *Hatfield, Herts*

8–13 June
1013 Russian – beginners   £200
Meirionnydd Languages
Trawsfynydd, North Wales

9–10 June
1014 Embroidery without kits   £AFD
Barn Crafts *Fincham, Norfolk*
Accommodation arranged on request.

9–11 June
1015 Speaking with
        confidence   £82
Lancashire College *Chorley*
ARCA

10–12 June
1016 Wines of the New World   £82
Lancashire College *Chorley*
ARCA

10–17 June
1017 Pembrokeshire Coast
        National Park   £209/268
Field Studies Council at Dale Fort
Field Centre *Haverfordwest*

12–13 June
1018 Interior design on a
        budget   £AFD
Barn Crafts *Fincham, Norfolk*
Accommodation arranged on request.

12–14 June
1019 Fine art to fine felt   £75/100
1020 Music appreciation   £75/100
Alston Hall Residential College
Preston
ARCA

12–14 June
1021 De-mystifying modern
        music   £75/95
1022 Bobbin along with lace   £75/95
1023 Colour and light – a
        course for painters   £75/95
Belstead House *Ipswich*
ARCA

12–14 June
1024 String chamber music   £122/142
Benslow Music Trust *Hitchin*
ARCA

12–14 June
1025 Choral weekend   £AFD
Dartington Hall *Totnes, Devon*

12–14 June
1026 Pen and wash   £79/105
1027 Picture framing   £90/115
Dillington House *Ilminster*
ARCA

12–14 June
1028 Grasses and grassland
     ecology   £92/115
Field Studies Council at Flatford Mill
Field Centre *East Bergholt*

12–14 June
1029 British Dragonfly Society
     Weekend   £86/112
Field Studies Council at Juniper Hall
Field Centre *Dorking*

12–14 June
1030 Sedges   £85/115
1031 Sketching and painting
     with watercolour sticks
     or pencils   £75/105
1032 Trees and tree
     identification   £75/105
Field Studies Council at Preston
Montford Field Centre *Shrewsbury*

12–14 June
1033 Garden croquet   £AFD
1034 Ruskin lace   £AFD
1035 Poetry of Dylan Thomas   £AFD
Higham Hall *Cockermouth*
ARCA

12–14 June
1036 Advanced parchment
     craft   £86
1037 Lincs writers' network   £AFD
Horncastle College *Horncastle*
ARCA

12–14 June
1038 Greeks and Romans in
     the Holy Land   £AFD
1039 Investment for beginners   £92
1040 Intermediate acoustic
     guitar   £92
Knuston Hall *Irchester*
ARCA

12–14 June
1041 Gold thread embroidery   £96
1042 Top to toe summer hair
     and beauty   £96
1043 Dowsing and divining   £96
1044 Window boxes/hanging
     baskets   £96
1045 Keep fit for the summer   £96
Lancashire College *Chorley*
ARCA

12–14 June
1046 Englishman discover the
     world: 1500–1700   £99
Maryland College *Woburn*
ARCA

12–14 June
1047 History of opera: Handel
     and Italian opera series   £AFD
1048 Botanical illustration   £AFD
1049 Tucks and texture two!   £AFD
1050 Picturing blue   £AFD
1051 Crochet with colour and
     texture   £AFD
1052 German conversation –
     intermediate   £AFD
1053 French conversation –
     intermediate   £AFD
1054 Dreams – power and
     practice   £AFD
1055 Keyboarding leisure play:
     advanced   £AFD
1056 Preparing working
     designs C & G/BOCN   £AFD
Missenden Abbey *Great Missenden*
ARCA

12–14 June
1057 Upstairs, downstairs: a
     social history of the
     country house   £AFD
1058 Mozart in Prague   £AFD
1059 Summer in mixed media   £AFD
The Old Rectory *Fittleworth*
ARCA

12–14 June
1060 Keep fit   £AFD
1061 Sugarcraft – wedding
     cakes   £AFD
Pendrell Hall College *Staffs*
ARCA

12–14 June
1062 Heretics and crusaders
in Languedoc   £120
1063 Aspects of Romanticism   £120
1064 Impressionist gardens   £120
1065 Birds in East Anglia   £120
Univ Cambridge *Madingley Hall*

12–14 June
1066 Greeks and Romans in
the Holy Land   £AFD
Univ Nottingham *Knuston Hall*

12–14 June
1067 Creative quilting   £85
1068 German conversation:
intermediate   £85
Wansfell College *Theydon Bois*
ARCA

12–14 June
1069 Rags to riches:
imaginative rag rugs   £70
1070 The Bronte legend   £70
Wedgwood Memorial College
Barlaston
ARCA

12–14 June
1071 The ornamental herb
garden   £AFD
1072 Batik – exploration   £AFD
1073 Stained glass   £AFD
1074 Bead making for
jewellery   £AFD
1075 Turner at Petworth –
lectures and practical
studies   £AFD
1076 Woodcarving   £AFD
1077 Decorative tassels and
cords   £AFD
West Dean College *Chichester*
ARCA

12–15 June
1078 Geranium and
Ranunculus   £101/135
Field Studies Council at Slapton Ley
Field Centre *Kingsbridge, Devon*

12–15 June
1079 Charlotte Brontë and
Shirley   £AFD
Univ Nottingham *Bradford*

12–19 June
1080 Wild flowers   £216/280
Field Studies Council at Juniper Hall
Field Centre *Dorking*

12–19 June
1081 Papermaking   £AFD
Wye Valley Arts Centre *St. Briavel's,
Glos*
ARCA

13–14 June
1082 Garden design   £100
1083 Silk painting   £100
1084 Pottery   £100
Acorn Activities *Herefordshire,
Shropshire and Wales*

13–14 June
1085 Lichens   £38
Field Studies Council at Epping Forest
Field Centre *Loughton, Essex*

13–19 June
1086 Flower arranging   £414
HF Holidays *Bourton-on-the-Water*
1087 Arran's summer wildlife   £369
HF Holidays *Isle of Arran*
1088 Dvorak on Dvorak and
friends   £319
HF Holidays *Dovedale*
1089 Discover Dorset's local
history   £369
HF Holidays *Lyme Regis*

14–17 June
1090 Decorative tassels, cords
and woven braids   £AFD
West Dean College *Chichester*
ARCA

14–19 June
1091 Progressive painting   £AFD
Higham Hall *Cockermouth*
ARCA

14–19 June
1092 Mouldmaking and
casting for sculpture   £AFD
1093 Flower studies in
watercolour   £AFD
West Dean College *Chichester*
ARCA

14–19 June
1094 Chinese brush painting £AFD
Wye Valley Arts Centre *St. Briavel's, Glos*
ARCA

14–20 June
1095 Watercolour week £169/397
Weobley Art Centre *Weobley, Herefordshire*
ARCA

14–21 June
1096 Walking in the Lake
  District £AFD
Higham Hall *Cockermouth*
ARCA

15–19 June
1097 Summer school of
  pastoral theology £199
Carberry *Musselburgh, Edinburgh*

15–19 June
1098 Tapestry weaving £AFD
Dartington Hall *Totnes, Devon*

15–19 June
1099 Steaming through
  Snowdonia £192/220
Field Studies Council at
Rhyd-y-creuau *Betws-y-coed*

15–19 June
1100 Arts summer school £82
Lancashire College *Chorley*
ARCA

15–19 June
1101 Porcelain restoration –
  advanced £255
Mowbray School of Porcelain
Restoration *Hatfield, Herts*

15–19 June
1102 Landscape in
  watercolour £AFD
1103 Walking the Downs and
  Weald £AFD
1104 Stained glass making £AFD
The Old Rectory *Fittleworth*
ARCA

15–19 June
1105 Houses and gardens of
  Gloucestershire and the
  Cotswolds £439
Univ Birmingham *Dumbleton, Worcs*

16–17 June
1106 Enamelling pictures £AFD
Barn Crafts *Fincham, Norfolk*
Accommodation arranged on request.

18–21 June
1107 Elgar summer school £124
The Hill Residential Centre ,
Abergavenny
ARCA

19–20 June
1108 Life drawing £AFD
Barn Crafts *Fincham, Norfolk*
Accommodation arranged on request.

19–20 June
1109 Shiatsu £96
Lancashire College *Chorley*
ARCA

19–20 June
1110 Calligraphy £99
1111 A fresh look at
  Beethoven's music for
  solo piano £99
Maryland College *Woburn*
ARCA

19–21 June
1112 Cultural heritage
  weekend £175
1113 Industrial archaeology
  and social history £AFD
Acorn Activities *Herefordshire,
Shropshire and Wales*

19–21 June
1114 Houses of the Ribble
  valley £75/100
1115 Drawing for the terrified £75/100
Alston Hall Residential College
Preston
ARCA

19–21 June
1116 Christ, stress and glory
(Christ centred
management of stress) £AFD
1117 What kind of unity? – a
look at church unity £69
Ammerdown Centre *Radstock, Bath*

19–21 June
1118 Folk singing £75/95
1119 Rag rugs with a
difference £75/95
Belstead House *Ipswich*
ARCA

19–21 June
1120 String chamber music £85/105
Benslow Music Trust *Hitchin*
ARCA

19–21 June
1121 Classical guitar
workshop £98
Burton Manor College *South Wirral*
ARCA

19–21 June
1122 Design for knitting £AFD
1123 Painting Dartington £AFD
1124 Conversations with
chaos £AFD
Dartington Hall *Totnes, Devon*

19–21 June
1125 Water plants £92/115
1126 Drawing, sketching and
watercolours –
improvers £82/105
1127 Watercolour for absolute
beginners £82/105
Field Studies Council at Flatford Mill
Field Centre *East Bergholt*

19–21 June
1128 Practical Ayerveda £AFD
Hawkwood College *Stroud, Glos*
ARCA

19–21 June
1129 Continental flower
arranging £AFD
Higham Hall *Cockermouth*
ARCA

19–21 June
1130 Jane Austen at Bath £98
1131 Beginners bridge £88
1132 Yoga £88
1133 Placenames and
landscapes £88
The Hill Residential Centre
Abergavenny
ARCA

19–21 June
1134 Creative lacemaking £86
1135 Summer flowers in
watercolour £86
1136 Lincolnshire churches £96
1137 Silk ribbon flowers £86
Horncastle College *Horncastle*
ARCA

19–21 June
1138 C & G lace – I and II £83
1139 Northamptonshire
families £AFD
1140 Ancient Egypt £92
Knuston Hall *Irchester*
ARCA

19–21 June
1141 The art of bonsai £96
1142 Chinese £96
1143 Chinese brush painting £96
1144 Japanese £96
Lancashire College *Chorley*
ARCA

19–21 June
Craft Fair Weekend
1145 Everyone can sing £AFD
1146 Modern painting series –
surrealism £AFD
1147 Bags of beads £AFD
1148 Bobbin lacemaking –
Bucks point,
Bedfordshire and
Torchon £AFD
1149 Life class: Chinese style
Qu Lei Lei £AFD
1150 Shiatsu and Alexander
Technique £AFD
1151 Miniature furniture £AFD

19–21 June continued

1152   Things your creative writing tutor never told you   £AFD

1153   The art of creating joy   £AFD

Missenden Abbey *Great Missenden*
ARCA

19–21 June

1154   Domestic architecture of the arts and crafts movement   £120

1155   Virginia Woolf: three more novels   £120

1156   In praise of flowers   £120

1157   Politics of the parish in early-modern England   £120

Univ Cambridge *Madingley Hall*

19–21 June

1158   Flowers of coast and marshland   £AFD

Univ Nottingham *Gibraltar Point Field Station*

1159   Welsh National Opera: *Tosca* and *La Traviata*   £AFD

Univ Nottingham *Llandudno*

1160   Historic houses and families of Northamptonshire   £AFD

Univ Nottingham *Knuston Hall*

19–21 June

1161   Choral weekend   £AFD

1162   Machine knitting   £AFD

Urchfont Manor College *Devizes*
ARCA

19–21 June

1163   Summer piano music   £85

Wansfell College *Theydon Bois*
ARCA

19–21 June

1164   Die Grosse Flatter – German through literature   £74

1165   Circle dance   £70

Wedgwood Memorial College
Barlaston
ARCA

19–21 June

1166   Watercolour painting – ships, sea and sand   £84

1167   Richard Wagner: life and music   £84

Wensum Lodge *Norwich*
ARCA

19–21 June

1168   Mounting and framing pictures   £AFD

1169   Calligraphy   £AFD

1170   Paper embellishment for jewellery and other creative uses   £AFD

1171   Writing for the press – news and features   £AFD

1172   Watercolour for not quite beginners   £AFD

1173   Botanical illustration   £AFD

West Dean College *Chichester*
ARCA

19–21 June

1174   Tai-Chi   £AFD

1175   Beginners' drawing and monoprinting   £AFD

Wye Valley Arts Centre *St. Briavel's, Glos*
ARCA

19–22 June

1176   Black and white photography   £AFD

West Dean College *Chichester*
ARCA

19–26 June

1177   Embroidery summer school   £AFD

1178   Landscape and seascape painting in watercolour   £AFD

1179   China painting   £AFD

The Old Rectory *Fittleworth*
ARCA

20–21 June

1180   Gourmet cooking   £120

1181   Silversmithing and jewellery   £120

Acorn Activities *Herefordshire, Shropshire and Wales*

20–21 June
1182 Grass identification,
ecology and
management £38
**Field Studies Council at Epping Forest
Field Centre** *Loughton, Essex*

20–23 June
1183 Walking in North Wales
and the Borders £147
Burton Manor College *South Wirral*
ARCA

20–26 June
1184 Welsh National Opera £414
HF Holidays *Conwy*
1185 Drawing for beginners £414
1186 Choral singing £389
HF Holidays *Bourton-on-the-Water*
1187 Railways in the scenic
North West £469
HF Holidays *Coniston Water*

20–26 June
1188 Victorian narrative
painting £430
1189 Botanical illustration –
drawing and painting
summer flowers £430
Summer Academy *Univ Sheffield*
1190 Scottish landscape
painting £395
Summer Academy *Univ Stirling*

21–26 June
1191 Walking with a
sketchbook £AFD
1192 History of transport £AFD
Higham Hall *Cockermouth*
ARCA

21–26 June
1193 Find your psyche
through creativity –
painting £AFD
1194 Portrait heads in
terracotta £AFD
1195 Portrait painting in oils £AFD
1196 Caring for furniture £AFD
West Dean College *Chichester*
ARCA

21–26 June
1197 Flowers in watercolour £AFD
Wye Valley Arts Centre *St. Briavel's,
Glos*
ARCA

21–27 June
1198 Pottery with other
activities £395
Acorn Activities *Herefordshire,
Shropshire and Wales*

22–23 June
1199 Beginners' art £147
Burton Manor College *South Wirral*
ARCA

22–23 June
1200 Practical drawing £AFD
Pendrell Hall College *Staffs*
ARCA

22–26 June
1201 Jewish Christian
summer school part 1 –
the world of the
psalmists £130
Ammerdown Centre *Radstock, Bath*

22–26 June
1202 Interior design £82
Lancashire College *Chorley*
ARCA

22–26 June
1203 Painting figures in the
landscape £AFD
Urchfont Manor College *Devizes*
ARCA

23–24 June
1204 Sculpture £AFD
Barn Crafts *Fincham, Norfolk
Accommodation arranged on request.*

24–26 June
1205 Embroidery £92
1206 Lacemaking for all £92
Knuston Hall *Irchester*
ARCA

25–26 June
1207 Dowsing and devining £AFD
Pendrell Hall College *Staffs*
ARCA

25–28 June
1208 Discovering Derbyshire's
 gardens   £261
Univ Birmingham *Chesterfield,
Derbyshire*

26–27 June
1209 Woodcarving –
 beginners   £AFD
Barn Crafts *Fincham, Norfolk*
Accommodation arranged on request.

26–28 June
1210 The art of performing
 Lieder   £75/100
Alston Hall Residential College
Preston
ARCA

26–28 June
1211 Jewish Christian
 summer school part 2 –
 creation and spirituality   £69
Ammerdown Centre *Radstock, Bath*

26–28 June
1212 Recorder consorts   £75/95
Belstead House *Ipswich*
ARCA

26–28 June
1213 Choral weekend   £95/115
1214 Harpsichord weekend   £100/120
Benslow Music Trust *Hitchin*
ARCA

26–28 June
1215 The marriage of music
 and dance   £98
Burton Manor College *South Wirral*
ARCA

26–28 June
1216 Painting   £AFD
1217 Struggle for prayer as a
 struggle for
 consciousness   £AFD
1218 Britain's railways in the
 age of steam   £AFD
Dartington Hall *Totnes, Devon*

26–28 June
1219 An invitation to croquet   £90/115
1220 Pharoah's workers   £79/105
1221 A chip off the old block
 (hat making)   £85/110
Dillington House *Ilminster*
ARCA

26–28 June
1222 Making your camera
 work for you   £82/105
1223 Drawing and painting
 wildlife   £92/115
1224 Suffolk's medieval
 houses   £82/105
1225 Summer wild flowers   £82/105
Field Studies Council at Flatford Mill
Field Centre *East Bergholt*

26–28 June
1226 Introducing insects   £78/102
1227 Understanding geology
 in south east England   £78/102
1228 Wild flowers for
 beginners   £82/105
Field Studies Council at Juniper Hall
Field Centre *Dorking*

26–28 June
1229 Alexander Technique   £AFD
Hawkwood College *Stroud, Glos*
ARCA

26–28 June
1230 Music appreciation   £AFD
Higham Hall *Cockermouth*
ARCA

26–28 June
1231 Art appreciation   £88
1232 Healthy lifestyles   £88
1233 Exploring Gwent   £98
1234 Landscape painting   £88
The Hill Residential Centre
Abergavenny
ARCA

26–28 June
1235 Embroidery   £92
1236 Lacemaking for all   £92
1237 Garden painting   £92
1238 Bridge for improvers   £92
1239 Wind band   £AFD
Knuston Hall *Irchester*
ARCA

26–28 June

1240	A history of Chorley	£96
1241	Stencilling	£96
1242	A spiritual programme for the Millennium	£96
1243	Assertiveness	£96
1244	Yoga	£96

Lancashire College *Chorley*
ARCA

26–28 June

1245	Basic bridge	£99
1246	Japanese interiors and gardens	£99

Maryland College *Woburn*
ARCA

26–28 June

1247	Sir Edward Elgar	£AFD
1248	Watercolours made easy	£AFD
1249	Calligraphy – introduction	£AFD
1250	Drawing methods of the master	£AFD
1251	Earth energies and human auras	£AFD
1252	Storytelling	£AFD
1253	Fibre based printing	£AFD
1254	C & G embroidery – part I	£AFD
1255	C & G patchwork and quilting	£AFD

Missenden Abbey *Great Missenden*
ARCA

26–28 June

1256	Basic china mending	£135

Mowbray School of Porcelain Restoration *Hatfield, Herts*

26–28 June

1257	Lace making	£AFD
1258	Oriental dancing: belly dancing, veil dance, Mongolian folk dance	£AFD
1259	Painting in watercolour	£AFD

The Old Rectory *Fittleworth*
ARCA

26–28 June

1260	Story of the English village	£AFD
1261	Pattern alterations	£AFD
1262	Pewtercraft	£AFD
1263	Spanish – beginners	£AFD

Pendrell Hall College *Staffs*
ARCA

26–28 June

1264	Natural history of bats	£120
1265	Discovering the East Anglian rural landscape 900–1200 AD	£120
1266	More popular song: musical links and meanderings	£120
1267	Painting and drawing flowers	£120

Univ Cambridge *Madingley Hall*

26–28 June

1268	Medieval King's Lynn	£AFD

Univ Nottingham *King's Lynn*

26–28 June

1269	A celebration of wine	£AFD

Urchfont Manor College *Devizes*
ARCA

26–28 June

1270	Life in Blighty	£85
1271	Fitness through movement exercise and dance with the Keep Fit Association	£85/92

Wansfell College *Theydon Bois*
ARCA

26–28 June

1272	Free-born Englishman – radicalism and democracy	£70
1273	Dreams – towards an understanding of Self	£70

Wedgwood Memorial College
Barlaston
ARCA

26–28 June
1274 Mosaic – further
techniques £AFD
1275 Silk painting £AFD
1276 Jewellery £AFD
1277 Drawing workshop –
perspective £AFD
1278 Hand colouring
photographs £AFD
1279 Pottery – throwing and
turning in porcelain £AFD
West Dean College *Chichester*
ARCA

26–28 June
1280 Botanical and
miniatures/painting and
drawing £AFD
Wye Valley Arts Centre *St. Briavel's,*
Glos
ARCA

27–28 June
1281 Flower arranging £100
Acorn Activities *Herefordshire,*
Shropshire and Wales

27–28 June
1282 Wicca – the old way in
the modern world £60
Mountain Hall *Queensbury*
Price includes tuition/lunches.
Accommodation/dinner, B/B £25 per
night.

27 June–3 July
1283 Geology of the Lake
District £379
HF Holidays *Derwentwater*
1284 Classic Cotswolds £449
HF Holidays *Bourton-on-the-Water*
1285 South Devon heritage £389
HF Holidays *Thurlestone Sands*
1286 Landscape photography £339
HF Holidays *Freshwater Bay*
1287 Waterways of peak and
plain £379
HF Holidays *Dovedale*

27 June–3 July
1288 Understanding
Scotland's history £395
Summer Academy *Univ Stirling*

27 June–4 July
1289 Mountain flowers £299
Scottish Field Studies Association
Kindrogan Field Centre Pitlochry

28–29 June
1290 Singing weekend £95
Sing for Pleasure *London Colney, St.*
Albans

28 June–2 July
1291 Wood engraving £AFD
West Dean College *Chichester*
ARCA

28 June–3 July
1292 Bobbin lacemaking £285
Dillington House *Ilminster*
ARCA

28 June–3 July
1293 More Wessex walks £AFD
Urchfont Manor College *Devizes*
ARCA

28 June–3 July
1294 Summer painting
workshop £AFD
1295 Silversmithing £AFD
1296 Cabinet making – part 2 £AFD
1297 Life drawing and painting £AFD
West Dean College *Chichester*
ARCA

28 June–3 July
1298 Watercolour painting £AFD
Wye Valley Arts Centre *St. Briavel's,*
Glos
ARCA

28 June–4 July
1299 Pottery with other
activities £395
Acorn Activities *Herefordshire,*
Shropshire and Wales

28 June–4 July
1300 Plants and flowers for
gardens and interiors £315
Dillington House *Ilminster*
ARCA

28 June–4 July
1301 Storytelling in
    organisations   £AFD
Hawkwood College *Stroud, Glos*
ARCA

28 June–5 July
1302 Painting with
    watercolour   £AFD
Higham Hall *Cockermouth*
ARCA

29 June–1 July
1303 Alexander Technique   £80/110
Alston Hall Residential College
Preston
ARCA

29 June–2 July
1304 Roman art and
    architecture   £137
1305 Life painting   £137
Wansfell College *Theydon Bois*
ARCA

29 June–3 July
1306 Silversmithing   £158
1307 Watercolour   £158
The Hill Residential Centre
Abergavenny
ARCA

29 June–3 July
1308 English gardens – visits
    and lectures   £280
Maryland College *Woburn*
ARCA

29 June–21 August
1309 An orientation to art and
    design   £1595
Central Saint Martins College of Art
and Design *London*
*Price includes tuition only. Some
courses also include material costs.*

30 June–1 July
1310 Life drawing   £AFD
Barn Crafts *Fincham, Norfolk*
Accommodation arranged on request.

■   ■   ■   ■

July 1998

□   □   □   □

July
1311 Surviving as a research
    student   £AFD
1312 Developing presentation
    skills   £AFD
1313 Post GCSE French   £AFD
1314 Introduction to German   £AFD
1315 Introduction to Spanish   £AFD
Univ Lancaster Summer School
Lancaster

1–31 July
1316 Bird watching   £45*
1317 Flower arranging   £50*
1318 Drawing, oil painting and
    watercolours   £40*
1319 Basket making with cane   £50*
1320 Rush seating   £45*
1321 Cane seating   £45*
1322 Needlecraft   £40*
1323 Pottery (any Thursday)   £50

1–13 July continued
1324 Rural surprises (any
    weekend: minimum of 6
    people)   £175
1325 Woodwork (any
    consecutive 3 days
    except Sunday)   £165
1326 Furniture restoration (any
    consecutive 3 days
    except Sunday)   £165
1327 Landscape painting (any
    Sunday/Friday)   £375
1328 Chair making (any
    Monday/Friday:
    minimum of 2 people)   £250
1329 Bookbinding (any
    Monday/Friday:
    minimum of 2 people)   £250
Acorn Activities *Herefordshire,
Shropshire and Wales*
**Per day. Bookings can be made for
any number of days.*

71

2–6 July
1330 Mountain flowers £150/194
1331 Secret gardens £150/194
Field Studies Council at Blencathra
Field Centre *Threlkeld, Keswick*

3–4 July
1332 Acrylics £AFD
Barn Crafts *Fincham, Norfolk*
Accommodation arranged on request.

3–5 July
1333 Make and fit a lined
waistcoat £75/100
1334 Folk dancing weekend £75/100
Alston Hall Residential College
Preston
ARCA

3–5 July
1335 Summer saxes £97/117
1336 Classical period piano £97/117
Benslow Music Trust *Hitchin*
ARCA

3–5 July
1337 Gaia theory £AFD
1338 Mixed media £AFD
1339 Living life creatively £AFD
Dartington Hall *Totnes, Devon*

3–5 July
1340 Wanders amongst wild
flowers £80/104
Field Studies Council at Castle Head
Field Centre *Grange-over-Sands*

3–5 July
1341 Botanical illustration –
beginners £82/105
1342 Walking in Constable
Country £82/105
Field Studies Council at
Flatford Mill Field Centre *East*
Bergholt

3–5 July
1343 Badgers and smaller
mammals £78/102
1344 Identifying grasses in
flower £78/102
1345 Painting and drawing
butterflies £88/112
Field Studies Council at Juniper Hall
Field Centre *Dorking*

3–5 July
1346 Algae £90/115
Field Studies Council at Malham Tarn
Field Centre *Settle, N Yorks*

3–5 July
1347 Botanical illustration £75/105
1348 Dragonflies and
damselflies £85/115
1349 Getting to grips with
grasses £85/115
1350 Pondweeds £85/115
Field Studies Council at Preston
Montford Field Centre *Shrewsbury*

3–5 July
1351 Orkney exploration £98
1352 Garden adventure £98
1353 Italian language £88
The Hill Residential Centre
Abergavenny
ARCA

3–5 July
1354 Watercolour – beginners £86
1355 Antiques – beginners £86
1356 Water wildlife £86
1357 Free machine
embroidery £86
Horncastle College *Horncastle*
ARCA

3–5 July
1358 Designing conflict
simulations £92
Knuston Hall *Irchester*
ARCA

3–5 July
1359 Braids, cords and tassels £96
1360 Machine embroidery £96
Lancashire College *Chorley*
ARCA

3–5 July
1361 Quilting £99
Maryland College *Woburn*
ARCA

3–5 July
1362	Mozart's last year	£AFD
1363	Still life painting: Matisse	£AFD
1364	Goldwork embroidery	£AFD
1365	Career and life painting	£AFD
1366	Social history: Mr Palmer bought me an antimacassar	£AFD
1367	Raffia hats	£AFD
1368	Touch wood: superstitions	£AFD
1369	C & G embroidery – II	£AFD

Missenden Abbey *Great Missenden*
ARCA

3–5 July
1370	Staffordshire gardens	£AFD
1371	Tai Chi Chuan	£AFD
1372	Stumpwork – basic figurines	£AFD

Pendrell Hall College *Staffs*
ARCA

3–5 July
1373	BSHP: Kierkegaard and freedom	£150
1374	Italian weekend	£120
1375	Sicily and Sardinia	£120

Univ Cambridge *Madingley Hall*

3–5 July
1376	Lost canals of the East Midlands	£AFD

Univ Nottingham *Nottingham*
1377	Haydn at Esterhaza	£AFD

Univ Nottingham *Wadham College Oxford*

3–5 July
1378	Workshop for singers	£91
1379	Lacemaking	£85

Wansfell College *Theydon Bois*
ARCA

3–5 July
1380	Idle or idyll – rural life in art and literature in Victorian England	£70
1381	Jazz on a summer's weekend	£70

Wedgwood Memorial College
Barlaston
ARCA

3–5 July
1382	Picture framing	£AFD
1383	Beginners' drawing – monoprinting	£AFD

Wye Valley Arts Centre *St. Briavel's, Glos*
ARCA

3–6 July
1384	Four great Yorkshire families	£AFD

Univ Nottingham *University College Scarborough*

3–10 July
1385	Watercolour workshop	£AFD
1386	Calligraphy summer school	£AFD
1387	Bellringing	£AFD

The Old Rectory *Fittleworth*
ARCA

4–5 July
1388	Woodturning	£100

Acorn Activities *Herefordshire, Shropshire and Wales*

4–5 July
Misbourne Weekend
1389	Hollow portrait heads	£AFD
1390	Antique furniture restoration	£AFD
1391	Way of the Chinese brush	£AFD
1392	Fibre dyeing using the microwave	£AFD
1393	Line dancing	£AFD
1394	Stained glass BOCN – beginners	£AFD
1395	Relief printmaking BOCN: abstracting or painting from nature	£AFD

Missenden Abbey *Great Missenden*
ARCA

4–5 July
1396	Astrology for beginners	£60

Mountain Hall *Queensbury*
Price includes tuition/lunches. Accommodation/dinner, B/B £25 per night.

4–10 July
1397	T'ai Chi and walking	£349

HF Holidays *Thurlestone Sands*

4–10 July continued
1398 Singing for fun   £315
HF Holidays *Freshwater Bay*
1399 Castles of South Wales   £429
HF Holidays *Brecon*

4–10 July
1400 Durham Cathedral:
     monastery and church   £430
1401 Houses and gardens of
     Northumbria   £430
Summer Academy *Univ Durham*
1402 The stately homes of
     Derbyshire   £430
Summer Academy *Univ Sheffield*
1403 Gilbert White and the
     landscapes of Wessex   £430
1404 The archaeology of
     Roman Wessex   £430
1405 Abbeys and cathedrals of
     Wessex   £430
1406 Spacetime and the
     shape of the Universe   £430
1407 The gardens of Wessex   £430
Summer Academy *Univ Southampton*

4–10 July
1408 Creative writing
     (introductory)   £195
Univ Edinburgh *Edinburgh*

4–11 July
1409 Summer birds in
     Scotland   £294
Scottish Field Studies Association
Kindrogan Field Centre Pitlochry

4–11 July
1410 Archaeology of the
     Orkneys   £760
Univ Nottingham *Kirkwall, Orkney*

4–17 July
1411 Scottish literature   £135/250
1412 Archaeology in Scotland   £395
Univ Edinburgh *Edinburgh*

4–24 July
1413 Scottish Gaelic
     (elementary to
     advanced)   £165/230
Univ Edinburgh *Edinburgh*

5–8 July
1414 China painting   £120/150
Alston Hall Residential College
Preston
ARCA

5–10 July
1415 Portrait painting   £250/300
Alston Hall Residential College
Preston
ARCA

5–10 July
1416 Batik and fabric painting   £AFD
Wye Valley Arts Centre *St. Briavel's, Glos*
ARCA

5–11 July
1417 Wet into wet watercolour   £AFD
1418 Landscape geography   £AFD
Higham Hall *Cockermouth*
ARCA

5–11 July
1419 Watercolours –
     beginners   £169/397
Weobley Art Centre *Weobley, Herefordshire*
ARCA

5–12 July
1420 Bookbinding including
     finishing work   £AFD
West Dean College *Chichester*
ARCA

6–8 July
1421 Drawing from observation   £85
1422 From page to screen:
     short stories   £85
Wansfell College *Theydon Bois*
ARCA

6–10 July
1423 Tudor music summer
     school   £215/225
Benslow Music Trust *Hitchin*
ARCA

6–10 July

1424	Designing bags	£175
1425	Find your psyche through creativity	£165
1426	Figure drawing for fashion design	£165
1427	Introduction to video	£295
1428	Scriptwriting for film and TV	£85
1429	Introduction to multimedia	£550
1430	Moving image on the Mac – animation and video	£575
1431	Imagination and colour in watercolour	£170
1432	Bronze casting	£255
1433	New innovations in CAD/CAM for textiles	£550
1434	Sound	£180
1435	Creating art for the Internet	£350
1436	The figure in painting	£185
1437	Apple Mac design for beginners	£525
1438	Fashion at CSM – the London context	£225
1439	Creativity workshop for designers	£125

Central Saint Martins College of Art and Design *London*
Price includes tuition only. Some courses also include material costs.

6–10 July
Summer school:

1440	Art and society in Byzantium	£275*
1441	Art in Florence and Siena in C14th	£275*
1442	C16th Renaissance art in northern Europe	£275*
1443	London's public architecture from C17th-C19th	£275*
1444	Pre-Raphaelitism and Aestheticism	£275*
1445	Garden history: Romans – C19th	£275*
1446	Going native: ideas of the primitive within modern art	£275*

Courtauld Institute of Art *London*
*per week.

6–10 July

1447	An introduction to NVC: grasses and woodlands	£175/225
1448	Wild flowers	£175/225

Field Studies Council at Preston
Montford Field Centre *Shrewsbury*

6–10 July

1449	Double exposure: methods of art	£88

The Hill Residential Centre *Abergavenny*
ARCA

6–10 July

1450	Literary trail – visits to the homes of Bunyan, Shaw, Milton, Cowper	£280

Maryland College *Woburn*
ARCA

6–10 July

1451	Porcelain restoration – beginners	£235

Mowbray School of Porcelain Restoration *Hatfield, Herts*

6–10 July

1452	A pianist's journey home	£250
1453	Ernest Hemingway: man and myth	£250

Univ Cambridge *Madingley Hall*

6–10 July

1454	Enhanced communication skills for professional development (neuro linguistic programming)	£AFD
1455	Expressive drawing and painting	£AFD
1456	Limited edition prints	£AFD
1457	Making stained glass windows	£AFD

Univ Middlesex Summer School *London*
Tuition only. Accommodation arranged on request.

6–10 July

1458	Piano playing course	£170

Wansfell College *Theydon Bois*
ARCA

77

6–11 July
1459 Welsh – beginners   £200
Meirionnydd Languages
Trawsfynydd, North Wales

6–11 July
1460 Northumbria in the age
      of the castle   £450
Univ Birmingham *Alnwick,*
Northumbria

6–13 July
1461 German language   £194
1462 Watercolour   £194
The Hill Residential Centre
Abergavenny
ARCA

6–17 July
1463 London theatre – plays in
      performance   £600
Birkbeck College Univ London
London

6–17 July
1464 English with art and
      design   £595
Central Saint Martins College of Art
and Design *London*
Price includes tuition only. Some
courses also include material costs.

6–17 July
1465 Computing for social
      scientists 1   £135
1466 Counselling in education £135
1467 Performance   £245
1468 Video workshop   £245
Univ Middlesex Summer School
London
Tuition only. Accommodation
arranged on request.

6–22 July
1469 Evening life drawing   £115
1470 Evening photography –
      beginners   £180
Central Saint Martins College of Art
and Design *London*
Price includes tuition only. Some
courses also include material costs.

6–24 July
1471 Tailoring   £395
Central Saint Martins College of Art
and Design *London*
Price includes tuition only. Some
courses also include material costs.

6–24 July
1472 Introduction to literature £245
Univ Middlesex Summer School
London
Tuition only. Accommodation
arranged on request.

6 July–12 August
1473 3D graphics
      programming in C   £245
1474 Building object oriented
      interfaces with C++   £245
1475 Business law   £245
1476 Case studies in Java   £245
1477 Company law   £245
1478 Computer simulation of
      electronics – introduction £245
1479 Desktop publishing   £245
1480 English for business
      communication (for
      non-native speakers)   £245
1481 Health and medicinal
      foods   £245
1482 Health education   £245
1483 Improving your French   £245
1484 Improving your Spanish £245
1485 Information for health £245
1486 Interactive multimedia £245
1487 French – intermediate   £245
1488 Introduction to business £245
1489 Desktop publishing and
      design   £245
1490 Introduction to
      distributed computing   £245
1491 Introduction to
      information technology   £245
1492 Introduction to media
      and cultural studies   £245
1493 Introduction to
      Portuguese   £245
1494 Introductory Spanish   £245
1495 Systems development
      management   £245
1496 The European Union   £245
1497 The history of London
      from 1850   £245

6 July–12 August continued
1498 Personal finance   £245
1499 Introduction to
    information technology   £245
1500 Learn easily, learn
    effectively   £135
Univ Middlesex Summer School
London
Tuition only. Accommodation
arranged on request.

7–8 July
1501 Sculpture   £AFD
Barn Crafts *Fincham, Norfolk*
Accommodation arranged on request.

7–8 July
1502 Farming and rights of
    way   £AFD
Field Studies Council at Preston
Montford Field Centre *Shrewsbury*

7–10 July
1503 Watercolour painting   £139
Lancashire College *Chorley*
ARCA

9–12 July
1504 New vocal repertory –
    C20th music   £AFD
West Dean College *Chichester*
ARCA

10–11 July
1505 Pottery   £100
Acorn Activities *Herefordshire,*
Shropshire and Wales

10–11 July
1506 Watercolour painting on
    location   £AFD
Barn Crafts *Fincham, Norfolk*
Accommodation arranged on request.

10–12 July
1507 Art appreciation   £75/100
1508 Embroidered fabric
    covered boxes   £75/100
1509 Painting weekend   £75/100
Alston Hall Residential College
Preston
ARCA

10–12 July
1510 Keep fit   £98
Burton Manor College *South Wirral*
ARCA

10–12 July
1511 Rock climbing   £96/120
Field Studies Council at Castle Head
Field Centre *Grange-over-Sands*

10–12 July
1512 Dragonflies   £92/115
1513 New approaches to
    watercolour   £82/105
Field Studies Council at Flatford Mill
Field Centre *East Bergholt*

10–12 July
1514 Introducing ants   £78/102
1515 Legumes   £89/115
1516 Woodland butterflies of
    south east England   £88/112
Field Studies Council at Juniper Hall
Field Centre *Dorking*

10–12 July
1517 Lace   £88
The Hill Residential Centre
Abergavenny
ARCA

10–12 July
1518 Northamptonshire
    kaleidoscope   £92
1519 The plays of Anton
    Chekhov   £AFD
1520 Non fiction writing   £92
1521 Fabric work   £92
Knuston Hall *Irchester*
ARCA

10–12 July
1522 East Midland bobbin
    lacemaking   £99
1523 The shaping of modern
    Spain   £99
1524 Saint-Saëns and Les Six   £99
Maryland College *Woburn*
ARCA

10–12 July continued

1525	Be your own financial adviser II	£AFD
1526	Watercolour – beginners	£AFD
1527	Embroidery: my favourite things	£AFD
1528	Rag rugs	£AFD
1529	English folk heroes	£AFD
1530	Writing comedy for television	£AFD
1531	Bags of beads	£AFD
1532	Home interior design C & G: introduction	£AFD

Missenden Abbey *Great Missenden*
ARCA

10–12 July

1533	Creative colour calligraphy	£AFD
1534	Landscape painting	£AFD
1535	Three great symphonies: an exploration of Sibelius, Copland and Elgar	£AFD
1536	Complementary therapies	£AFD

The Old Rectory *Fittleworth*
ARCA

10–12 July

1537	Personality and communication	£120
1538	Grasses and flowering plants	£120
1539	Apocalypse now	£120

Univ Cambridge *Madingley Hall*

10–12 July

1540	The plays of Anton Chekhov	£AFD

Univ Nottingham *Knuston Hall*
Wellingborough

10–12 July

1541	Picasso	£70
1542	Walking the moorlands	£70

Wedgwood Memorial College
Barlaston
ARCA

10–12 July

1543	Traditional upholstery	£AFD
1544	Calligraphy	£AFD
1545	Walling in flint and stone	£AFD
1546	Cane and rush seating	£AFD

West Dean College *Chichester*
ARCA

10–12 July

1547	Silk painting	£AFD

Wye Valley Arts Centre *St. Briavel's,*
Glos
ARCA

10–13 July

1548	Castles of medieval Gwent	£AFD

Univ Nottingham *UWCN Caerleon,*
Newport

10–14 July

1549	Pembrokeshire coast and offshore islands	£144/184

Field Studies Council at Dale Fort
Field Centre *Haverfordwest*

10–15 July

1550	Landscape painting	£255

Painting in Pembrokeshire *St. David's*

10–17 July

1551	French	£312

Lancashire College *Chorley*
ARCA

10–17 July

1552	Pre-Raphaelite week	£420

Univ Cambridge *Madingley Hall*

11–12 July

1553	Bridge for beginners	£80
1554	Silk painting	£100
1555	Stained glass	£120
1556	Drawing for the terrified	£96
1557	Photography	£120
1558	Rush seating	£90

Acorn Activities *Herefordshire,*
Shropshire and Wales

11–12 July

1559	Higher plant classification and identification	£38

Field Studies Council at Epping Forest
Field Centre *Loughton, Essex*

11–16 July
1560 Historic houses of
      Sussex   £499
HF Holidays *Abingworth*
1561 Preserved railways of
      South Wales   £499
HF Holidays *Brecon*

11–17 July
1562 Viol summer school   £249/295
Benslow Music Trust *Hitchin*
ARCA

11–17 July
1563 Enjoying music and
      walking   £369
HF Holidays *Derwentwater*
1564 Landscape photography   £389
HF Holidays *Dovedale*

11–17 July
1565 Now and then: a
      comparison of all kinds
      of classic and
      contemporary writing   £430
1566 English customs and
      traditions   £430
1567 In praise of trees   £430
Summer Academy *Univ Sheffield*
1568 Hadrian's Wall and the
      Roman army   £430
1569 Lords and commoners in
      the north east of England   £395
Summer Academy *Univ Durham*
1570 The peoples' past:
      Scotland before 1800   £395
Summer Academy *Univ Stirling*
1571 Insect diversity in South
      Wales   £395
Summer Academy *Univ Wales,
Swansea*

11–17 July
1572 Creative writing (short
      story)   £195
Univ Edinburgh *Edinburgh*

11–18 July
1573 Painting with
      watercolour   £AFD
1574 The Romans in the North   £AFD
Higham Hall *Cockermouth*
ARCA

11–18 July
1575 Summer painting   £283
1576 Natural history of the
      Highlands   £283
Scottish Field Studies Association
Kindrogan Field Centre Pitlochry

11 July–7 August
1577 Scotland through the
      ages (history, literature,
      art, architecture)   £160/580
Univ Edinburgh *Edinburgh*

12–17 July
1578 Country gardens   £229
Knuston Hall *Irchester*
ARCA

12–17 July
1579 Poetry masterclass:
      mapping the journey   £360
1580 Prose masterclass:
      getting it right   £360
Univ Cambridge *Madingley Hall*

12–17 July
1581 Mosaics in glass and
      ceramic   £AFD
1582 Silversmithing and
      jewellery   £AFD
1583 Traditional hand finishing   £AFD
1584 Botanical illustration   £AFD
1585 Flute master classes   £AFD
West Dean College *Chichester*
ARCA

12–17 July
1586 Watercolour painting   £AFD
Wye Valley Arts Centre *St. Briavel's,
Glos*
ARCA

12–18 July
1587 Pottery with other
      activities   £395
Acorn Activities *Herefordshire,
Shropshire and Wales*

12–18 July
1588 Pen and ink with
      watercolour   £169/397
Weobley Art Centre *Weobley,
Herefordshire*
ARCA

13–14 July
1589 Keep fit £AFD
Pendrell Hall College *Staffs*
ARCA

13–16 July
1590 Antiques £140
Burton Manor College *South Wirral*
ARCA

13–17 July
1591 Creativity for fine artists £125
1592 Millinery – beginners £175
1593 16mm film-making £650
1594 Jewellery making –
beginners £250
1595 Life drawing – beginners £160
1596 Magazine production and
design £525
1597 Drawing and painting the
head £185
1598 Oil painting course £185
1599 Photography – beginners £225
1600 Computer knit £380
1601 Gas welding £195
1602 Glass casting £255
1603 Greetings card
illustration £165
1604 Video as a source £235
1605 Developing artist
initiated independent
projects £80
1606 Issues in word and
image £100
1607 Electronic portfolio
development for artists £385
1608 DTP for web pages £550
1609 Moving image on the
Mac – 3D animation £575
**Central Saint Martins College of Art
and Design** *London*
*Price includes tuition only. Some
courses also include material costs.*

13–17 July
Summer school:
1610 Art and society in
Byzantium £275*
1611 Art in Florence and Siena
in C14th £275*
1612 C16th Renaissance art in
northern Europe £275*
1613 London's public
architecture from
C17th-C19th £275*

13–17 July continued
1614 Pre-Raphaelitism and
Aestheticism £275*
1615 Garden history: Romans
– C19th £275*
1616 Going native: ideas of
the primitive within
modern art £275*
Courtauld Institute of Art *London*
**per week.*

13–17 July
1617 Porcelain restoration –
intermediate £245
**Mowbray School of Porcelain
Restoration** *Hatfield, Herts*

13–17 July
1618 Introduction to
entomology £135
1619 Personal effectiveness £AFD
Univ Middlesex Summer School
London
*Tuition only. Accommodation
arranged on request.*

13–17 July
1620 Massage and relaxation £AFD
Urchfont Manor College *Devizes*
ARCA

13–17 July
1621 Scagliola part I £AFD
West Dean College *Chichester*
ARCA

13–18 July
1622 Painting all media £AFD
Knuston Hall *Irchester*
ARCA

13–19 July
1623 French £230
The Hill Residential Centre
Abergavenny
ARCA

14–15 July
1624 Embroidery without kits £AFD
Barn Crafts *Fincham, Norfolk*
Accommodation arranged on request.

QUALITY STUDY BREAKS
in England & Wales
AT PLACES OF CHARACTER AND HISTORIC INTEREST

ARCA is a well-established association of Residential Colleges for Adult Education. It provides a wide range of quality short-stay courses for the general public. Some colleges are run by local authorities; others by charitable trusts or similar organisations. All share a professional approach to education in a residential setting and are wholeheartedly committed to the principle of "life-long learning"; learning for personal satisfaction and enjoyment.

It is this liberal approach to learning that is at the heart of ARCA. You do not need academic qualifications to enrol; all you need do is complete a booking form and return it with your fee. Telephone bookings and credit card payments are accepted by many colleges.

Attending an ARCA college can be a simple pleasure or an event, which looking back, you may see as a turning point in your life. A short-stay course can lead on to a formal course of study and to a recognised qualification.

Each college publishes its own programme of courses and will be glad to send you a copy.

Members of the Adult Residential Colleges Association are listed on the following pages with their postal and e-mail addresses, and telephone numbers.
•
A World of Adult Learning is just a telephone call away!

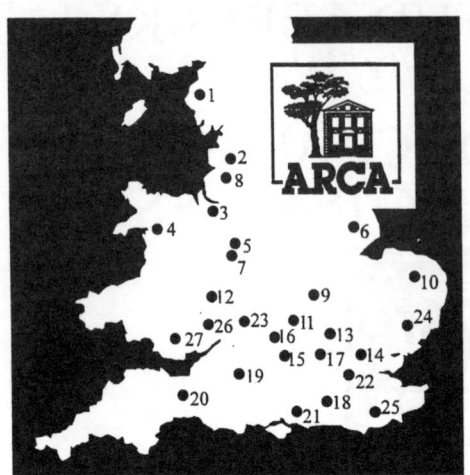

THE ARCA COLLEGES

1

Higham Hall, BASSENTHWAITE LAKE
Cockermouth , Cumbria CA13 9SH
Tel: 01768 776 276 Fax: 01768 776 013
e-mail: higham.hall@dial.pipex.com

2

Alston Hall College, LONGRIDGE,
Preston, Lancs PR3 3BP
Tel: 01772 784 661 Fax: 01772 785 835

3

Burton Manor College, BURTON,
South Wirral, Cheshire L64 5SJ
Tel: 0151 336 5172/3 Fax 0151 336 6586
e-mail: burton@lineone.net

4

Plas Tan y Bwlch; Snowdonia National Park
Study Centre, MAENTWROG, Blaenau
Ffestiniog, Gwynedd LL41 3YU
Tel: 01766 590 324 Fax: 01766 590 274
e-mail: plastanybwlch@compuserve.com

5

Wedgwood Memorial College, BARLASTON,
Stoke-on-Trent, Staffs ST12 9DG
Tel: 01782 372 105 Fax: 01782 372 393
e-mail: wedgwood.college@staffordshire.gov.uk

6

Horncastle College; Mareham Road,
HORNCASTLE, Lincs, LN9 6BW
Tel: 01507 522 449 Fax: 01507 524 382
e-mail:
horncastle.college@irac.org.uk

7

Pendrell Hall, CODSALL WOOD,
Wolverhampton, Staffs WV8 1QP
Tel 01902 434 112 Fax 01902 434 113
e-mail:
pendrell.college@staffordshire.gov.uk

8

Lancashire College, Southport Road,
CHORLEY, Lancashire PR7 1NB
Tel: 01257 276 719 Fax: 01257 241 370

9

Knuston Hall, IRCHESTER,
Wellingborough, Northants NN29 7EW
Tel: 01933 312 104 Fax: 01933 357 596
e-mail:
101346.1322@compuserve.com

10

Wensum Lodge, King Street, NORWICH,
Norfolk NR1 1QW
Tel: 01603 666 021 Fax: 01603 765 633
e-mail:
itstudy@netcom.co.uk

11

Maryland College, Leighton Street,
WOBURN, Beds MK17 9JD
Tel: 01525 292 901 Fax: 01525 290 058

12

Weobley Art Centre, The Old Corner
House, Broad Street, WEOBLEY,
Herefordshire HR4 8SA
Tel & Fax: 01544 318 548
e-mail:
enquiries@weobley.demon.co.uk

13

Benslow Music Trust, Little Benslow Hills,
Ibberson Way, HITCHIN, Herts SG4 9RB
Tel: 01462 459 446 Fax:01462 440 171

14
Wansfell College, 30 Piercing Hill,
THEYDON BOIS, Epping, Essex CM16 7LF
Tel: 01992 813 027 Fax:01992 814 761
e-mail:
marilyntaylor@essexcc.gov.uk

15
Braziers; IPSDEN, Wallingford, Oxon
OX10 6AN
Tel: 01491 680 221

16
Denman College, MARCHAM, Abingdon,
Oxon OX13 6NW
Tel: 01865 391 991 Fax: 01865 391 966

17
Missenden Abbey: GREAT MISSENDEN,
Bucks HP16 0BD
Tel: 01494 890 295/6 Fax: 01494 863 697
e-mail:
enquiries@missendenabbey.ac.uk

18
The Old Rectory Adult Education College,
FITTLEWORTH, Pulborough, W.Sussex
RH20 1HU
Tel & Fax: 01798 865 306
e-mail: oldrectory@mistral.co.uk

19
Urchfont Manor, URCHFONT, Nr. Devizes,
Wiltshire SN10 4RG
Tel: 01380 840 495 Fax 01380 840 005

20
Dillington House, ILMINSTER, Somerset
TA19 9DT
Tel: 01460 52427 Fax: 01460 52433

21
West Dean College, WEST DEAN,
Chichester, Sussex PO18 0QZ
Tel: 01243 811 301 Fax: 01243 811 343
e-mail:
westdean@pavilion.co.uk

22
Debden House, Debden Green, LOUGHTON,
Essex IG10 2PA
Tel: 0181 508 3008 Fax: 0181 508 0284

23
Hawkwood College, Painswick Old Road,
STROUD, Gloucestershire GL6 7QW
Tel: 01453 759 034 Fax: 01453 764 607
e-mail: hawkwood@compuserve.com

24
Belstead House, Belstead, IPSWICH,
Suffolk IP8 3NA
Tel: 01473 686 321 Fax: 01473 686 664

25
Pyke House, Upper Lake, BATTLE, East
Sussex TN33 0AN
Tel: 01424 772 495 Fax: 01424 775 041

26
Wye Valley Arts Centre, Mork, St. Briavels,
LYDNEY, Gloucestershire GL15 6QH
Tel: 01594 530 214 Fax: 01594 530 321

27
The Hill Residential Centre, Pen-y-Pound,
ABERGAVENNY, Gwent NP7 7RP
Tel: 01495 333 777 Fax: 01495 333 778

ADULT RESIDENTIAL COLLEGES ASSOCIATION

Secretary: Derek Barbanell,
Church Lane, Washbrook, Ipswich IP8 3HF

Visit the
ARCA Website
at
http://www.aredu.demon.co.uk

THE ARCA SYMBOL IS YOUR SIGN OF QUALITY

ARCA colleges share an atmosphere unlike that of other educational institutions. Many are historic houses set in beautiful countryside, far from the pressures and distractions of everyday life; others may be Victorian or Edwardian family homes. However stately or modest their location, ARCA colleges proudly maintain a high standard in hospitality and tuition which is regularly monitored by the association.

Regular ARCA monitoring is your guarantee of quality in what is probably the best residential adult education in the country.

Fees vary from college to college. The comfortable accommodation may be simple or grandly en-suite. Staff are supportive and always ready to help. Most dietary needs can be supplied and many colleges offer facilities for people with disabilities.

Attending a short-stay residential course is a wonderful way of meeting new people. Through repeat visits strong friendships can form and regular learning breaks at ARCA colleges can easily become a way of life!

Adult Residential Colleges Association

14–17 July
1625 Golf intermediate – short
game special   £166
Knuston Hall *Irchester*
ARCA

16–19 July
1626 Christ stress and glory
(Christ centred
management of stress)   £AFD
Ammerdown Centre *Radstock, Bath*

17–18 July
1627 Beadwork   £90
Acorn Activities *Herefordshire,
Shropshire and Wales*

17–18 July
1628 Interior design on a
budget   £AFD
Barn Crafts *Fincham, Norfolk
Accommodation arranged on request.*

17–19 July
1629 Drawing for the terrified   £75/100
1630 Honiton lacemaking   £75/100
Alston Hall Residential College
Preston
ARCA

17–19 July
1631 Male ferns   £90/114
Field Studies Council at Blencathra
Field Centre *Threlkeld, Keswick*

17–19 July
1632 In search of the Red Kite £80/107
1633 Water plants   £85/115
Field Studies Council at Preston
Montford Field Centre *Shrewsbury*

17–19 July
1634 Out and about with a
sketchbook   £88
1635 Parchment craft   £88
The Hill Residential Centre
Abergavenny
ARCA

17–19 July
1636 The World Wide Web for
business or pleasure   £92
1637 Golf for beginners   £122
Knuston Hall *Irchester*
ARCA

17–19 July
1638 Summer house party   £99
1639 Water colour for
beginners   £99
Maryland College *Woburn*
ARCA

17–19 July
1640 Mozart operas   £120
Univ Cambridge *Madingley Hall*

17–19 July
1641 Medieval books to 1500:
production and use   £AFD
Univ Nottingham *Lucy Cavendish
College Cambridge*
1642 Moths and butterflies   £AFD
Univ Nottingham *Gibraltar Point Field
Station*

17–19 July
1643 Ways with watercolour   £70
1644 Meditation to quieten
the mind   £70
Wedgwood Memorial College
Barlaston
ARCA

17–19 July
1645 Colour in the garden   £AFD
1646 Punch and toolmaking
for chasing and repousse   £AFD
1647 Botanical illustration   £AFD
West Dean College *Chichester*
ARCA

17–19 July
1648 Chinese brush painting   £AFD
Wye Valley Arts Centre *St. Briavel's,
Glos*
ARCA

17–20 July
1649 Butterflies and moths   £110/140
1650 Improve your botany:
daisies, dandelions and
thistles   £115/145
1651 Improve your oil
painting   £110/140
Field Studies Council at Flatford Mill
Field Centre *East Bergholt*

17–21 July
1652 High peaks   £141/185
Field Studies Council at Blencathra
Field Centre *Threlkeld, Keswick*

17–24 July
1653 Discovering Lakeland
          landscape   £205/268
1654 Introducing geology   £205/268
Field Studies Council at Blencathra
Field Centre *Threlkeld, Keswick*

17–24 July
1655 Improve your
          watercolours   £221/280
Field Studies Council at Flatford Mill
Field Centre *East Bergholt*

17–24 July
1656 Scenery and geology in
          the Borderlands   £190/255
Field Studies Council at Preston
Montford Field Centre *Shrewsbury*

17–24 July
1657 Woodcarving summer
          school   £AFD
1658 Walking and sketching   £AFD
The Old Rectory *Fittleworth*
ARCA

17–24 July
1659 Film studies: 2 courses £120/250
Univ Cambridge *Madingley Hall*

18–19 July
1660 Drystone walling   £80
1661 Organic kitchen
          gardening   £80
1662 Calligraphy   £90
1663 Camcorder and video
          skills   £120
1664 Interior design   £90
1665 Basket making with
          English willow   £100
1666 Cane seating   £90
1667 Spinning   £100
1668 Weaving   £100
1669 Sculpture   £120
Acorn Activities *Herefordshire,
Shropshire and Wales*

18–19 July
1670 Palmistry – hand analysis   £60
Mountain Hall *Queensbury*
*Price includes tuition/lunches.
Accommodation/dinner, B/B £25 per
night.*

18–20 July
1671 Mah Jong – beginners   £AFD
Knuston Hall *Irchester*
ARCA

18–21 July
1672 Introducing grasses   £136
Scottish Field Studies Association
Kindrogan Field Centre Pitlochry

18–24 July
1673 Literature summer
          school   £AFD
Ammerdown Centre *Radstock, Bath*

18–24 July
1674 String quartet summer
          school   £230/270
Benslow Music Trust *Hitchin*
ARCA

18–24 July
1675 Glass, lakes and steam   £460
1676 Women in medieval life
          and literature   £395
Summer Academy *Univ Kent,
Canterbury*
1677 Landscape and geology
          of the north   £395
1678 Celtic dawn, Roman
          morn and Anglo-Saxon
          noon II   £430
Summer Academy *Univ Durham*
1679 The world of Jane
          Austen   £430
1680 Rituals, shrines and
          sacrifice in Roman
          Britain   £430
1681 Wildlife in the Exe
          estuary   £430
Summer Academy *Univ Exeter*
1682 Churches of East Anglia   £430
1683 Windmills and
          waterways   £430
Summer Academy *Univ East Anglia,
Norwich*

18–24 July continued
1684 Exploring Scotland's old
    burghs   £395
Summer Academy *Univ Stirling*
1685 Dylan Thomas – *When I
    was young and easy*   £395
Summer Academy *Univ Wales,
Swansea*

18–24 July
1686 Presentation skills   £150
1687 Nature conservation in
    Scotland   £180
Univ Edinburgh *Edinburgh*

18–24 July
1688 Chilingirian string quartet   £AFD
West Dean College *Chichester*
ARCA

18–25 July
1689 Multi-art and craft week   £450
Acorn Activities *Herefordshire,
Shropshire and Wales*

18–25 July
1690 Landscape and/or flower
    painting   £AFD
Higham Hall *Cockermouth*
ARCA

18–31 July
1691 Creative writing
    (playwriting)   £345
Univ Edinburgh *Edinburgh*

18 July–1 August
1692 Westonbirt summer
    school   £330*
Birkbeck College *Westonbirt, Glos*
*per week.

19–22 July
1693 Stained glass   £AFD
West Dean College *Chichester*
ARCA

19–23 July
1694 Scagliola part II   £AFD
West Dean College *Chichester*
ARCA

19–24 July
1695 Music appreciation   £250/300
Alston Hall Residential College
Preston
ARCA

19–24 July
1696 A view of ancient
    Suffolk   £170/220
1697 Gardens of East Anglia   £170/220
Belstead House *Ipswich*
ARCA

19–24 July
1698 Bridge   £AFD
Higham Hall *Cockermouth*
ARCA

19–24 July
1699 Wagner – *The Ring*   £229
Knuston Hall *Irchester*
ARCA

19–24 July
1700 Painting summer school   £AFD
Pendrell Hall College *Staffs*
ARCA

19–24 July
1701 Graining, marbling and
    decorative paint
    techniques   £AFD
West Dean College *Chichester*
ARCA

19–24 July
1702 Botanical and miniatures
    – painting and drawing   £AFD
Wye Valley Arts Centre *St. Briavel's,
Glos*
ARCA

19–25 July
1703 Pottery with other
    activities   £395
Acorn Activities *Herefordshire,
Shropshire and Wales*

19–25 July
1704 Successful writing   £315
Dillington House *Ilminster*
ARCA

19 July–1 August
1705 Summer workshop in
     Greek and Latin   £175*
Univ of Wales *Lampeter*
*price per week.

20–22 July
1706 Summer flower
     arranging   £86
1707 Creative landscape
     painting   £86
1708 China for the tea table   £86
Horncastle College *Horncastle*
ARCA

20–23 July
1709 This year's Proms   £127
1710 Practical painting   £127
1711 Epping and Hainault
     Forests   £137
Wansfell College *Theydon Bois*
ARCA

20–24 July
1712 Health studies   £176
Burton Manor College *South Wirral*
ARCA

20–24 July
1713 Illustrating with the Mac   £525
1714 Computers for fine
     artists   £350
1715 Interior design   £165
1716 Design for menswear   £160
1717 Children's book
     illustration   £165
1718 Metal workshop   £190
1719 Drawing from the dance   £185
1720 Interactive multimedia –
     a complete production   £550
1721 Urban landscape
     watercolour painting   £155
1722 Portrait photography   £225
1723 Drawing portfolio   £150
1724 An experience of art
     school   £190
1725 Fashion design using
     heat transfer printing   £435

20–24 July continued
1726 Millinery – open
     workshop   £175
1727 Fashion knit   £225
1728 Computers for fashion   £330
1729 Publishing on the
     Internet – a guide for
     teachers   £275
**Central Saint Martins College of Art
and Design** *London*
*Price includes tuition only. Some
courses also include material costs.*

20–24 July
1730 Creative calligraphy
     week   £142/180
1731 Garden flowers and
     garden design   £142/180
1732 Improve your pastel
     painting   £142/180
**Field Studies Council at Flatford Mill
Field Centre** *East Bergholt*

20–24 July
1733 Family wildlife discovery
     week   £AFD
**Field Studies Council at Juniper Hall
Field Centre** *Dorking*

20–24 July
1734 China painting   £172
1735 Open art workshop   £AFD
1736 Pots, plants and
     porcelain   £86
1737 Hand painted silk with
     hand and m/c quilting   £86
1738 Silversmithing   £86
Horncastle College *Horncastle*
ARCA

20–24 July
1739 Machine embroidery   £200
1740 Summer watercolour
     painting   £200
Maryland College *Woburn*
ARCA

20–24 July
1741 Porcelain restoration –
     advanced   £255
**Mowbray School of Porcelain
Restoration** *Hatfield, Herts*

20–24 July
1742 Botanical illustration   £250
1743 Recording a medieval
     village   £250
Univ Cambridge *Madingley Hall*

20–24 July
1744 Environmental ecology
     field course   £AFD
Univ Middlesex Summer School
London
*Tuition only. Accommodation
arranged on request.*

20–24 July
1745 Fabric dyeing and
     printing   £AFD
Urchfont Manor College *Devizes*
ARCA

20–27 July
1746 Nature photography in
     high summer   £218/275
**Field Studies Council at Juniper Hall
Field Centre** *Dorking*

20–31 July
1747 Art history and English   £445
**Central Saint Martins College of Art
and Design** *London*
*Price includes tuition only. Some
courses also include material costs.*

20–31 July
1748 Computing for social
     scientists 2   £245
Univ Middlesex Summer School
London
*Tuition only. Accommodation
arranged on request.*

21–22 July
1749 Enamelling pictures   £AFD
Barn Crafts *Fincham, Norfolk*
Accommodation arranged on request.

21–24 July
1750 Wetlands, woodlands
     and wild places   £112/148
**Field Studies Council at Blencathra
Field Centre** *Threlkeld, Keswick*

21–24 July
1751 Country garden style   £AFD
West Dean College *Chichester*
ARCA

21–25 July
1752 An introduction to
     national vegetation
     classification   £205
Scottish Field Studies Association
Kindrogan Field Centre Pitlochry

22–29 July
1753 Summer painting in and
     around Nettlecombe   £187/247
**Field Studies Council at Nettlecombe
Court** *Taunton, Somerset*

22–29 July
1754 Black and white
     landscape photography £210/270
1755 Exploring the
     Pembrokeshire Coast
     National Park   £200/260
**Field Studies Council at Orielton Field
Centre** *Pembroke*

23–26 July
1756 Neuro-linguistic
     programming – diploma
     intensive   £230
Mountain Hall *Queensbury*
*Price includes tuition/lunches.
Accommodation/dinner, B/B £25 per
night.*

24–25 July
1757 Basket making with cane   £100
Acorn Activities *Herefordshire,
Shropshire and Wales*

24–25 July
1758 Life drawing   £AFD
Barn Crafts *Fincham, Norfolk*
Accommodation arranged on request.

24–26 July
1759 Folk dance   £98
Burton Manor College *South Wirral*
ARCA

24–26 July
1760 Have a go at caving   £96/120
**Field Studies Council at Castle Head
Field Centre** *Grange-over-Sands*

24–26 July
1761 Butterflies, birds and
     other flying creatures   £88/112
Field Studies Council at Juniper Hall
Field Centre *Dorking*

24–26 July
1762 Basic botany for
     gardeners   £75/105
1763 Identifying ferns   £75/105
1764 Understanding scenery
     in the south Shropshire
     hills   £75/105
1765 Wild plants and wild
     places: Shropshire's
     secret garden   £85/115
Field Studies Council at Preston
Montford Field Centre *Shrewsbury*

24–26 July
1766 Look out for mammals:
     an identification
     workshop   £50/90
1767 Butterflies and moths   £79/105
1768 Nocturnal natural history:
     badgers and bats   £79/105
Field Studies Council at Slapton Ley
Field Centre *Kingsbridge, Devon*

24–26 July
1769 Lacemaking –
     Bedfordshire   £92
1770 Lacemaking – design   £92
1771 Studying old lace   £92
1772 Needle lace   £92
Knuston Hall *Irchester*
ARCA

24–26 July
1773 Tassles for furniture and
     jewellery   £99
1774 Jane Austen and Mrs
     Gaskell   £99
1775 *King Lear* – practical
     reading and
     dramatisation   £99
Maryland College *Woburn*
ARCA

24–26 July
1776 Flowers in watercolour
     and gouache   £AFD
1777 Close harmony and
     barbershop   £AFD
1778 Computer course   £AFD
The Old Rectory *Fittleworth*
ARCA

24–26 July
1779 Découpage   £AFD
1780 China painting   £AFD
1781 Writing – a practical
     guide   £AFD
Pendrell Hall College *Staffs*
ARCA

24–26 July
1782 The vernacular
     architecture of the
     Chilterns   £167
Univ Birmingham *Chalfont St. Giles,
Buckinghamshire*

24–26 July
1783 Beside the seaside   £AFD
Univ Nottingham *Gibraltar Point Field
Station*

24–26 July
1784 Conversational French   £70
1785 Planet earth –
     preservation weekend   £70
Wedgwood Memorial College
Barlaston
ARCA

24–27 July
1786 Batik and silk painting –
     beginners   £110/140
1787 Introducing invertebrate
     biodiversity   £110/140
1788 Painting in pastels for
     beginners   £110/140
Field Studies Council at Flatford Mill
Field Centre *East Bergholt*

24–31 July
1789 Marquetry   £223/293
1790 Calligraphy   £223/293
Belstead House *Ipswich*
ARCA

24–31 July
1791 Grasses, sedges and
      rushes   £222/285
1792 Landscape painting and
      drawing   £205/268
1793 Lichens: introducing their
      ecology and
      identification   £205/268
**Field Studies Council at Blencathra
Field Centre** *Threlkeld, Keswick*

24–31 July
1794 Improve your
      watercolours   £221/280
**Field Studies Council at Flatford Mill
Field Centre** *East Bergholt*

24–31 July
1795 Insects   £216/280
**Field Studies Council at Juniper Hall
Field Centre** *Dorking*

24–31 July
1796 Fly fishing in the
      Yorkshire Dales   £200/270
1797 Grasses, sedges and
      rushes   £200/270
**Field Studies Council at Malham Tarn
Field Centre** *Settle, N Yorks*

24–31 July
1798 Ecology and
      management of organic
      gardens and wildlife
      habitats   £185/262
**Field Studies Council at
Rhyd-y-creuau** *Betws-y-coed*

24–31 July
1799 Landscape through
      painting and sculpture   £195/260
1800 Tai Chi: inspiration from
      nature   £195/260
**Field Studies Council at Slapton Ley
Field Centre** *Kingsbridge, Devon*

24–31 July
1801 Orchestral summer
      school   £AFD
Hawkwood College *Stroud, Glos*
ARCA

24–31 July
1802 German   £312
Lancashire College *Chorley*
ARCA

24–31 July
1803 Alberni   £390
Univ Cambridge *Madingley Hall*

24–31 July
1804 Landscape for beginners   £AFD
Wye Valley Arts Centre *St. Briavel's,
Glos*
ARCA

25–26 July
1805 Silversmithing and
      jewellery   £120
1806 Flower arranging   £100
1807 Spinning   £100
1808 Weaving   £100
Acorn Activities *Herefordshire,
Shropshire and Wales*

25–26 July
1809 Chi Kung   £60
Mountain Hall *Queensbury*
*Price includes tuition/lunches.
Accommodation/dinner, B/B £25 per
night.*

25–31 July
1810 Mountain leader
      training   £237/295
**Field Studies Council at
Rhyd-y-creuau** *Betws-y-coed*

25–31 July
1811 Earth energy   £349
HF Holidays *Lyme Regis*
1812 Harrogate International
      Festival   £469
HF Holidays *Malhamdale*
1813 Get going – get fit   £399
HF Holidays *Whitby*
1814 Music making for
      orchestra and choir   £369
HF Holidays *Selworthy*
1815 Gilbert and Sullivan   £394
1816 The re-birth of our
      railways   £499
HF Holidays *Bourton-on-the-Water*

25–31 July

1817   Wool, silk and linen thread: fabric makers in Kent and their communities   £430

1818   The origins of Christianity in Britain   £430

Summer Academy *Univ Kent, Canterbury*

1819   Industrial archaeology of the North   £395

1820   Hadrian's Wall and the Roman army   £430

Summer Academy *Univ Durham*

1821   The country house in the South West   £430

1822   Rise of the Devon seaside resorts   £430

1823   The once and future king: the evolution of Arthurian legends   £430

Summer Academy *Univ Exeter*

1824   The country houses of Lancashire   £430

1825   Popular piety: the Reformation and the monasteries   £430

1826   Antiques and implements of Georgian times   £430

1827   Three magic operas   £430

Summer Academy *Univ Lancaster*

1828   East Anglian market towns   £430

1829   East Anglian peculiarities: flowering fens, barren brecks and a shingle spit   £430

Summer Academy *Univ East Anglia, Norwich*

1830   The history and treasures of Oxford University   £460

1831   Shakespeare's romantic comedies   £460

1832   Oxford at war: the local community in the English Civil War   £460

Summer Academy *Keble College Oxford*

1833   The wild wood of Scotland   £395

Summer Academy *Univ Stirling*

25–31 July

1834   Our global environment   £135

Univ Edinburgh *Edinburgh*

25–31 July

1835   Creative photography workshop   £AFD

1836   Silk painting – Indian influences   £AFD

1837   Summer watercolours   £AFD

1838   Making jewellery   £AFD

1839   Drawing and painting landscape towards abstraction   £AFD

1840   Rag rugs and wallhangings   £AFD

1841   Pottery including Raku and stoneware glaze firings   £AFD

West Dean College *Chichester* ARCA

25 July–1 August

1842   Chamber music   £250/300

Alston Hall Residential College *Preston* ARCA

25 July–1 August

1843   Painting and prayer   £210

Ammerdown Centre *Radstock, Bath*

25 July–1 August

1844   Carberry Festival (week 'A')*   £155

Carberry *Musselburgh, Edinburgh*
suitable for family groups.

25 July–1 August

1845   Welsh for learners   £250

1846   French for learners   £250

Coleg Harlech *Harlech*

25 July–1 August

1847   Patchwork   £AFD

1848   Painting vibrancy in colour   £AFD

Higham Hall *Cockermouth* ARCA

25 July–1 August

| 1849 | Capturing the magic of gardens (photography) | £305 |
| 1850 | Freshwater algae | £335 |

Scottish Field Studies Association
Kindrogan Field Centre Pitlochry

25 July–2 August

| 1851 | Geology and scenery of the Pembrokeshire coast | £209/268 |

Field Studies Council at Dale Fort Field Centre *Haverfordwest*

25 July–2 August

| 1852 | Scottish architecture | £180/320 |

Univ Edinburgh *Edinburgh*

25 July–14 August

| 1853 | Drama from page from stage | £340* |

Univ Edinburgh *Edinburgh*
*includes theatre tickets.

26–30 July

| 1854 | Harp summer school | £210* |

Benslow Music Trust *Hitchin*
ARCA
*resident only.

26–31 July

| 1855 | Discovery and adventure | £AFD |

Field Studies Council at Castle Head Field Centre *Grange-over-Sands*

26–31 July

| 1856 | Exploring landscapes from Dartmoor to the coast | £131/175 |
| 1857 | Ecological biology of ferns | £131/175 |

Field Studies Council at Slapton Ley Field Centre *Kingsbridge, Devon*

26–31 July

1858	Lacemaking – Bedfordshire	£229
1859	Lacemaking – Bedfordshire (beginners)	£229
1860	Lacemaking – Whitof and Duchesse	£229
1861	Lacemaking – Tambor/Limmerick	£229

Knuston Hall *Irchester*
ARCA

26 July–1 August

| 1862 | Norman knights and castles | £315 |
| 1863 | Photography | £315 |

Dillington House *Ilminster*
ARCA

26 July–1 August

1864	Batik and painting on silk	£109
1865	Bird watching	£139
1866	Computing	£89
1867	Creative writing	£69
1868	Croquet	£89
1869	Golf	£209
1870	History	£139
1871	Languages for pleasure	£69
1872	Music	£69
1873	Painting and drawing	£99
1874	Philosophy	£69
1875	Rambles	£79

Univ Lancaster Summer School
Lancaster

26 July–1 August

| 1876 | Watercolour week | £169/397 |

Weobley Art Centre *Weobley, Herefordshire*
ARCA

27–29 July

1877	Contemporary calligraphy	£86
1878	Furniture restoration	£86
1879	Creating with stained glass	£86

Horncastle College *Horncastle*
ARCA

27–29 July

| 1880 | Exploring chamber music | £AFD |

Pendrell Hall College *Staffs*
ARCA

27–30 July

| 1881 | Bookbinding and repairs | £127 |
| 1882 | Photography | £175 |

Wansfell College *Theydon Bois*
ARCA

27–31 July

| 1883 | Bookbinding | £250 |

Acorn Activities *Herefordshire, Shropshire and Wales*

27–31 July
1884 Alexander Technique   £190
Burton Manor College *South Wirral*
ARCA

27–31 July
1885 Apple Mac for beginners   £525
1886 Drawing – introduction   £155
1887 Pattern cutting for
      menswear and
      womenswear   £275
1888 Making, editing,
      producing video   £575
1889 Intermediate jewellery   £250
1890 Why nude?   £170
1891 Painting – beginners   £155
1892 Landscape photography   £225
1893 Foundation drawing
      school   £130
1894 Computer design for
      textiles   £330
1895 Creative constructed
      textiles   £225
1896 Stained glass   £335
1897 Digital video: type and
      the moving image   £550
1898 Working in television   £85
1899 Technical skills in interior
      design   £165
1900 Professional training for
      computer graphics   £240
1901 Creating interactive
      CD-Roms   £550
1902 Model-making and basic
      moulds   £185
**Central Saint Martins College of Art
and Design** *London*
*Price includes tuition only. Some
courses also include material costs.*

27–31 July
1903 Creative writing   £142/180
1904 Drawing and painting
      wildlife for families
      (YOC)   £AFD
1905 Flatford family wildlife
      week   £AFD
**Field Studies Council at Flatford Mill
Field Centre** *East Bergholt*

27–31 July
1906 Embroidery   £158
The Hill Residential Centre
Abergavenny
ARCA

27–31 July
1907 Woodcarving   £200
1908 Visits to places of
      interest in Bedfordshire
      and Buckinghamshire   £280
Maryland College *Woburn*
ARCA

27–31 July
1909 Chinese brush painting   £AFD
1910 Sugarcraft   £AFD
Pendrell Hall College *Staffs*
ARCA

27–31 July
1911 The World Wide Web in
      a week   £245
Univ Middlesex Summer School
London
*Tuition only. Accommodation
arranged on request.*

27–31 July
1912 Historic monuments in
      the Scottish Borders   £AFD
Univ Nottingham *Dumfries*

27–31 July
1913 Bookbinding and book
      restoration   £AFD
Urchfont Manor College *Devizes*
ARCA

27 July–2 August
1914 Exhibitions   £AFD
Burton Manor College *South Wirral*
ARCA

27 July–2 August
1915 Welsh language   £230
The Hill Residential Centre
Abergavenny
ARCA

27 July–7 August
1916 Graphics summer school   £360
**Central Saint Martins College of Art
and Design** *London*
*Price includes tuition only. Some
courses also include material costs.*

27 July–7 August
1917 Permaculture design　　　£245
1918 Approaches to physical
　　theatre　　　　　　　£AFD
Univ Middlesex Summer School
London
Tuition only. Accommodation
arranged on request.

28–29 July
1919 Longbow making　　　£AFD
Barn Crafts *Fincham, Norfolk*
Accommodation arranged on request.

28–30 July
1920 Ruskin lace　　　　　£82
Lancashire College *Chorley*
ARCA

28 July–1 August
1921 Bugs, beasts and birds
　　(YOC)　　　　　　£AFD
Field Studies Council at Dale Fort
Field Centre *Haverfordwest*

29–31 July
1922 Calligraphy – illuminated
　　initials　　　　　　£86
1923 Upholstery　　　　　£86
1924 Creating with stained
　　glass　　　　　　£86
Horncastle College *Horncastle*
ARCA

29 July–5 August
1925 Landscape drawing and
　　painting　　　　£187/247
Field Studies Council at Nettlecombe
Court *Taunton, Somerset*

29 July–5 August
1926 Walking the
　　Pembrokeshire coast　£200/260
Field Studies Council at Orielton Field
Centre *Pembroke*

31 July–1 August
1927 Acrylics　　　　　£AFD
Barn Crafts *Fincham, Norfolk*
Accommodation arranged on request.

31 July–2 August
1928 Environmental art　£86/110
Field Studies Council at Castle Head
Field Centre *Grange-over-Sands*

31 July–2 August
1929 National Vegetation
　　Classification (NVC)　£92/115
Field Studies Council at Flatford Mill
Field Centre *East Bergholt*

31 July–2 August
1930 Look out for mammals:
　　an identification
　　workshop　　　　£50/90
1931 An inordinate fondness
　　for beetles　　　£85/115
1932 Roman Shropshire　£75/105
Field Studies Council at Preston
Montford Field Centre *Shrewsbury*

31 July–2 August
1933 Lacemaking –
　　Bedfordshire (beginners)　£92
1934 Watercolour – beginners　£92
Knuston Hall *Irchester*
ARCA

31 July–2 August
1935 Tai Chi Chuan　　　£96
Lancashire College *Chorley*
ARCA

31 July–2 August
1936 Making sense of modern
　　art　　　　　　£99
1937 Bedfordshire's
　　environmental heritage　£99
Maryland College *Woburn*
ARCA

31 July–2 August
1938 T'ai Chi Chuan　　　£AFD
1939 Life and art in C18th
　　England　　　　£AFD
1940 Painting course　　£AFD
The Old Rectory *Fittleworth*
ARCA

31 July–2 August
1941 The symphonic poem –
　　in theory and practice　£120
1942 Archaeological
　　techniques for local
　　historians　　　　£120
1943 The road to Santiago and
　　Muslim Spain　　　£120
1944 C19th Writing　　　£120
Univ Cambridge *Madingley Hall*

101

31 July–2 August
1945 To win a war? – the German offensives on the Western Front in the spring and summer of 1918: an 80th anniversary re-appraisal   £125
Univ Birmingham *Ludlow, Shropshire*

31 July–2 August
1946 Historic gardens of bath   £AFD
1947 Stonehenge revisited   £AFD
Urchfont Manor College *Devizes*
ARCA

31 July–2 August
1948 Beginners' drawing and monoprinting   £AFD
1949 Picture framing   £AFD
Wye Valley Arts Centre *St. Briavel's, Glos*
ARCA

31 July–3 August
1950 Making your camera work for you   £110/140
1951 Summer birdwatching   £110/140
Field Studies Council at Flatford Mill Field Centre *East Bergholt*

31 July–4 August
1952 Diving the Skomer Marine Reserve and Pembrokeshire Islands   £160/205
Field Studies Council at Dale Fort Field Centre *Haverfordwest*

31 July–7 August
1953 Needlecrafts   £223/293
1954 Painting   £223/293
1955 Summer music   £223/293
1956 Go-it-alone lace   £167/237
Belstead House *Ipswich*
ARCA

31 July–7 August
1957 Improve your watercolours   £221/280
Field Studies Council at Flatford Mill Field Centre *East Bergholt*

31 July–7 August
1958 Trees   £216/280
Field Studies Council at Juniper Hall Field Centre *Dorking*

31 July–7 August
1959 Butterflies and moths   £200/270
1960 Fens and bogs: the ecology of peatlands   £200/270
Field Studies Council at Malham Tarn Field Centre *Settle, N Yorks*

31 July–7 August
1961 Drawing and painting in all media   £190/255
1962 Mosses and liverworts   £200/280
1963 Pictures for your portfolio   £195/265
Field Studies Council at Preston Montford Field Centre *Shrewsbury*

31 July–7 August
1964 Landscape painting in Snowdonia   £185/262
1965 Snowdonia National Park exploration   £185/262
1966 Wild flowers of Snowdonia and the North Wales coast   £185/262
Field Studies Council at Rhyd-y-creuau *Betws-y-coed*

■ ■ ■ ■

August 1998

☐ ☐ ☐ ☐

August
1967	Writing a dissertation	£AFD
1968	Time management	£AFD
1969	Stress management	£AFD
1970	Report writing	£AFD
1971	Communication skills	£AFD
1972	Assertiveness training	£AFD
1973	Advice and guidance	£AFD
1974	Presenting yourself with confidence	£AFD
1975	Introduction to word processing	£AFD
1976	Introduction to Excel	£AFD
1977	Introduction to the Internet	£AFD
1978	Writing Web pages	£AFD
1979	Computing in context	£AFD
1980	Introduction to databases using Access	£AFD
1981	Multi media applications	£AFD
1982	Digital imaging	£AFD

Univ Lancaster Summer School *Lancaster*

1–2 August
1983	Woodturning	£100
1984	Watercolour for the terrified	£96
1985	Papier mâché	£90
1986	Pottery	£100

Acorn Activities *Herefordshire, Shropshire and Wales*

1–5 August
1987	Habitats and their conservation	£144/184
1988	Seascapes: exploring the Pembrokeshire coast	£144/184

Field Studies Council at Dale Fort Field Centre *Haverfordwest*

1–7 August
1989	Flower arranging	£364

HF Holidays *St Ives*

1–7 August
1990	Exploring the gardens of Kent	£460
1991	Kent: geology, landscape and wildlife	£460

Summer Academy *Univ Kent, Canterbury*
1992	Northumbrian Christianity	£430
1993	Finding a voice	£370

Summer Academy *Univ Durham*
1994	Romantic poets in the West Country	£430
1995	West Country churches	£430
1996	Alfred the Great and Vikings in south west England	£430

Summer Academy *Univ Exeter*
1997	Changing face of Norfolk's villages	£430
1998	East Anglia and its art	£430

Summer Academy *Univ East Anglia, Norwich*
1999	History and treasures of Oxford University	£460
2000	Gothic revival: art and architecture in Victorian England	£460
2001	Making of Oxford's gardens	£460

Summer Academy *Keble College Oxford*
2002	Roman Britain	£430
2003	Exploring ancient churches and their symbolism	£430
2004	Decorative textiles: from C16th lace to C20th embroidery	£430

Summer Academy *Univ Sheffield*
2005	Scotland's hidden history	£395

Summer Academy *Univ Stirling*

1–7 August
2006	Waterways summer school	£280

Wedgwood Memorial College *Barlaston*
ARCA

1–7 August

2007	Enamelling techniques in jewellery making and smallwork on silver or copper	£AFD
2008	Stone carving – sculptural contrasts	£AFD
2009	Handbuilding ceramics	£AFD
2010	Mosaics in marble, glass and stone	£AFD
2011	Hand knitting – exploring colour, texture and pattern	£AFD
2012	Drawing from the model	£AFD
2013	Light and atmosphere in watercolour	£AFD

West Dean College *Chichester*
ARCA

1–8 August

2014	Baltimore quilting	£250/300
2015	Painting and drawing	£250/300

Alston Hall Residential College
Preston
ARCA

1–8 August

2016	Carberry Festival (week 'B')*	£155

Carberry *Musselburgh, Edinburgh*
**suitable for family groups.*

1–8 August

2017	Landscape painting	£250
2018	Time to read	£250
2019	Hill walking	£250
2020	Welsh homes and gardens	£250
2021	Writers' workshop	£250
2022	Sign language	£250
2023	Counselling skills	£250
2024	Preparing for higher education	£250
2025	Wales and Europe	£250

Coleg Harlech *Harlech*

1–8 August

2026	Taste of Pembrokeshire: history, nature, photography and more	£209/268

Field Studies Council at Dale Fort
Field Centre *Haverfordwest*

1–8 August

2027	Botanical illustration	£AFD
2028	Bridge and walking	£AFD

Higham Hall *Cockermouth*
ARCA

1–8 August

2029	Photographing insects	£299
2030	Grasses	£294

Scottish Field Studies Association
Kindrogan Field Centre Pitlochry

1–14 August

2031	Film studies	£205
2032	Scottish folk life studies	£485

Univ Edinburgh *Edinburgh*

1–31 August

2033	Bird watching	£45*
2034	Flower arranging	£50*
2035	Drawing, oil painting and watercolours	£40*
2036	Basket making with cane	£50*
2037	Rush seating	£45*
2038	Cane seating	£45*
2039	Needlecraft	£40*
2040	Pottery (any Thursday)	£50
2041	Rural surprises (any weekend: minimum of 6 people)	£175
2042	Woodwork (any consecutive 3 days except Sunday)	£165
2043	Furniture restoration (any consecutive 3 days except Sunday)	£165
2044	Landscape painting (any Sunday/Friday)	£375
2045	Chair making (any Monday/Friday: minimum of 2 people)	£250
2046	Bookbinding (any Monday/Friday: minimum of 2 people)	£250

Acorn Activities *Herefordshire, Shropshire and Wales*
**Per day. Bookings can be made for any number of days.*

2–7 August

2047	Big band summer school	£225/265

Benslow Music Trust *Hitchin*
ARCA

2–7 August

2048 Discovery and adventure   £AFD
**Field Studies Council at Castle Head
Field Centre** *Grange-over-Sands*

2–7 August

2049 Mountain leader
     assessment   £228/270
**Field Studies Council at
Rhyd-y-creuau** *Betws-y-coed*

2–7 August

2050 Exploring watercolour
     techniques   £229
Knuston Hall *Irchester*
ARCA

2–8 August

2051 Guitar summer school   £AFD
Dillington House *Ilminster*
ARCA

2–8 August

2052	Bowls	£250/345
2053	Horse riding	£250/345
2054	Golf	£250/345
2055	Fitness, sport and adventure	£250/345
2056	Coast and country walks	£250/345
2057	Exploring the Quantocks	£250/345
2058	Hunkypunks and crocketed pinnacles	£250/345
2059	Somerset villages	£250/345
2060	Artists in Somerset	£250/345
2061	Arts a la carte	£250/345
2062	Private gardens	£250/345
2063	English country house	£250/345
2064	Antiques	£250/345
2065	Introduction to drawing and painting	£250/345
2066	Stained glass	£250/345
2067	Travels with your camera	£250/345
2068	Silverwork	£250/345
2069	Papier mache	£250/345
2070	Calligraphy	£250/345
2071	Art: working from the figure	£250/345

2–8 August continued

2072	Woodturning	£250/345
2073	Music and computers	£250/345
2074	Choral singing	£250/345
2075	Make piano your forte	£250/345
2076	Alexander Technique	£250/345
2077	Sense and nonsense in civilisation	£250/345
2078	Traveller's Spanish	£250/345
2079	Face reading	£250/345
2080	Computers (TSS Website)	£250/345
2081	Creative writing	£250/345
2082	Appearance matters	£250/345
2083	Speak with confidence	£250/345
2084	Design your own garden	£250/345
2085	Investment for beginners	£250/345

Taunton Summer School *Taunton*
All holidays open to family groups.

2–8 August

2086 Watercolour week   £169/397
Weobley Art Centre *Weobley,
Herefordshire*
ARCA

2–9 August

2087 Watercolour painting   £AFD
Wye Valley Arts Centre *St. Briavel's,
Glos*
ARCA

3–5 August

2088 Woodturning   £86
2089 Woodcarving   £86
2090 Dressmaking –
     beginners   £86
Horncastle College *Horncastle*
ARCA

3–5 August

2091 Early C20th writing   £120
2092 The naughty nineties:
     life, culture and society
     in Britain 1890–1900   £120
Univ Cambridge *Madingley Hall*

3–6 August

2093 Complementary
     therapies   £139
Lancashire College *Chorley*
ARCA

3–7 August
2094 Calligraphy £190
Burton Manor College *South Wirral*
ARCA

3–7 August
2095 3 dimensional design
computer graphics
modelling £380
2096 Introduction to
QuarkXPress and
photoshop £525
2097 Creativity and self
expression £225
2098 Total drawing £150
2099 Approaches to painting £185
2100 Portrait painting £185
2101 Art workshop for 16–18s £155
2102 Bridal wear £160
2103 Old photographic printing
processes £295
2104 Landscape design £165
2105 The naked body £180
Central Saint Martins College of Art
and Design *London*
Price includes tuition only. Some
courses also include material costs.

3–7 August
2106 Exploring Suffolk £142/180
2107 Flatford family wildlife
week £AFD
2108 Illustrating animals £142/180
Field Studies Council at Flatford Mill
Field Centre *East Bergholt*

3–7 August
2109 Family wildlife discovery
week £AFD
Field Studies Council at Juniper Hall
Field Centre *Dorking*

3–7 August
2110 Creative art £AFD
2111 The wonders of nature £AFD
Field Studies Council at Preston
Montford Field Centre *Shrewsbury*

3–7 August
2112 Crochet £158
2113 Spanish language £158
2114 Landscape in
watercolour £230
The Hill Residential Centre
Abergavenny
ARCA

3–7 August
2115 Life and landscape
painting £188
Horncastle College *Horncastle*
ARCA

3–7 August
2116 Landscape painting in oil £200
Maryland College *Woburn*
ARCA

3–7 August
2117 Upholstery, chair caning
and seagrass £AFD
2118 Landscape painting in
watercolour £AFD
2119 Exploring early Sussex £AFD
The Old Rectory *Fittleworth*
ARCA

3–7 August
2120 Some views of
philosophy £250
Univ Cambridge *Madingley Hall*

3–7 August
2121 Drawing and painting for
the petrified II £AFD
Urchfont Manor College *Devizes*
ARCA

3–8 August
2122 Russian – beginners £200
Meirionnydd Languages
Trawsfynydd, North Wales

3–9 August
2123 Writers £230
The Hill Residential Centre
Abergavenny
ARCA

4–5 August
2124 Sculpture £AFD
Barn Crafts *Fincham, Norfolk*
Accommodation arranged on request.

5–7 August
2125	Woodturning – improvers	£86
2126	Woodcarving	£86
2127	Bridge	£86
2128	Win cars, cash, cruises	£86

Horncastle College *Horncastle*
ARCA

5–7 August
| 2129 | Contemporary writing | £120 |
| 2130 | Life and leisure in Edwardian England, 1900–1914 | £120 |

Univ Cambridge *Madingley Hall*

5–12 August
2131	Birds and butterflies in high summer	£208/268
2132	Landscape drawing and painting	£187/247
2133	Painting plants and flowers	£187/247

Field Studies Council at Nettlecombe
Court *Taunton, Somerset*

6–8 August
| 2134 | Wildlife weekend – Pembrokeshire | £150 |

Acorn Activities *Herefordshire,*
Shropshire and Wales

6–13 August
| 2135 | Radius summer school | £AFD |

Radius, Queen's College *Edgbaston*

7–8 August
| 2136 | Watercolour painting on location | £AFD |

Barn Crafts *Fincham, Norfolk*
Accommodation arranged on request.

7–9 August
| 2137 | Banjo weekend | £85/105 |

Benslow Music Trust *Hitchin*
ARCA

7–9 August
| 2138 | Bats | £99/125 |

Field Studies Council at Flatford Mill
Field Centre *East Bergholt*

7–9 August
| 2139 | Wildlife photography | £88/112 |

Field Studies Council at Juniper Hall
Field Centre *Dorking*

7–9 August
| 2140 | Umbellifers | £85/115 |

Field Studies Council at Preston
Montford Field Centre *Shrewsbury*

7–9 August
| 2141 | Dragonflies and hoppers | £79/105 |

Field Studies Council at Slapton Ley
Field Centre *Kingsbridge, Devon*

7–9 August
2142	Folk summer school	£92
2143	Spanish literature	£92
2144	Embroidery	£92
2145	Silversmithing and jewellery making	£92

Knuston Hall *Irchester*
ARCA

7–9 August
| 2146 | Wildlife television – an insider's story | £99 |
| 2147 | English parish churches | £99 |

Maryland College *Woburn*
ARCA

7–9 August
2148	Oriental dancing	£AFD
2149	Map and compass for walkers	£AFD
2150	Wine appreciation weekend	£AFD
2151	Painting course	£AFD

The Old Rectory *Fittleworth*
ARCA

7–9 August
2152	Trends in domestic architecture	£120
2153	The portrait in the Italian Renaissance	£120
2154	Japanese architecture, gardens and tea culture	£120

Univ Cambridge *Madingley Hall*

7–9 August
| 2155 | Investigating crop circles | £AFD |
| 2156 | Decorative folk art | £AFD |

Urchfont Manor College *Devizes*
ARCA

7–10 August
2157 Walking back in time:
         history through the
         landscape   £110/140
Field Studies Council at Flatford Mill
Field Centre *East Bergholt*

7–10 August
2158 Otters   £100/135
Field Studies Council at Preston
Montford Field Centre *Shrewsbury*

7–14 August
2159 Botanising in south
         Lakeland: taxonomy and
         techniques   £198/268
2160 Discovery and adventure   £AFD
Field Studies Council at Castle Head
Field Centre *Grange-over-Sands*

7–14 August
2161 Botanical illustration –
         advanced   £221/280
2162 Painting in Constable
         Country – beginners and
         improvers   £221/280
Field Studies Council at Flatford Mill
Field Centre *East Bergholt*

7–14 August
2163 Outdoor painting   £195/270
2164 Walking in Shropshire £140/245
Field Studies Council at Preston
Montford Field Centre *Shrewsbury*

7–14 August
2165 Decorative hand
         marbling   £199/265
2166 Churches of South
         Devon   £195/260
2167 Rural rambles: green
         lanes to village inns £218/290
2168 Silk screen printing £214/285
Field Studies Council at Slapton Ley
Field Centre *Kingsbridge, Devon*

8–9 August
2169 Self-development
         through Tarot and
         astrology   £60
Mountain Hall *Queensbury*
Price includes tuition/lunches.
Accommodation/dinner, B/B £25 per
night.

8–11 August
2170 Understanding
         computing for
         beginners   £111/142
Field Studies Council at Dale Fort
Field Centre *Haverfordwest*

8–13 August
2171 The healing elements of
         Pembrokeshire   £160/205
Field Studies Council at Dale Fort
Field Centre *Haverfordwest*

8–14 August
2172 Kingdom of Northumbria   £409
HF Holidays *Alnmouth*
2173 Music making for
         orchestra and choir   £414
HF Holidays *Malhamdale*

8–14 August
2174 History of the Cinque
         Ports   £430
2175 Kent houses and their
         families   £460
Summer Academy *Univ Kent,
Canterbury*
2176 Northumbrian churches   £395
2177 The English town and
         village: Anglo-Saxon
         Viking and Norman   £395
Summer Academy *Univ Durham*
2178 East Anglian market
         towns   £430
2179 Country house in East
         Anglia   £430
Summer Academy *Univ East Anglia,
Norwich*
2180 History and treasures of
         Oxford University   £460
2181 Shakespeare's romantic
         comedies   £460
2182 Making of Oxford's
         gardens   £460
Summer Academy *Keble College
Oxford*
2183 A shipbuilding history of
         Scotland   £460
2184 Charles Rennie
         Mackintosh and the
         Glasgow style   £460
Summer Academy *Univ Strathclyde,
Glasgow*

8–14 August continued
2185 William Burges and the
     Gothic revival   £430
Summer Academy *Univ Wales,*
Swansea

8–14 August
2186 Summer painting   £220
Wedgwood Memorial College
Barlaston
ARCA

8–14 August
2187 Lettering and language in
     art and craft   £AFD
2188 Sculptural ceramics   £AFD
2189 General oil painting   £AFD
2190 Enamelling, art and craft   £AFD
2191 Expressive and
     adventurous colour in
     painting   £AFD
2192 Creative tapestry
     weaving   £AFD
2193 Creative blacksmithing   £AFD
2194 Experimental stitched
     textiles   £AFD
West Dean College *Chichester*
ARCA

8–15 August
2195 Multi art and craft week   £450
Acorn Activities *Herefordshire,*
Shropshire and Wales

8–15 August
2196 Orchestral playing   £270
Coleg Harlech *Harlech*

8–15 August
2197 Creatures great and
     small: mammals of the
     Lake District   £212/275
2198 Lakeland valley walks   £212/275
2199 Landscape painting in
     watercolours   £205/268
Field Studies Council at Blencathra
Field Centre *Threlkeld, Keswick*

8–15 August
2200 Jazz performance   £AFD
Higham Hall *Cockermouth*
ARCA

9–14 August
2201 Calligraphy   £320
Dillington House *Ilminster*
ARCA

9–14 August
2202 Bird migration in South
     Devon   £131/175
Field Studies Council at Slapton Ley
Field Centre *Kingsbridge, Devon*

9–14 August
2203 Embroidery   £229
2204 Silversmithing and
     jewellery making   £229
2205 Music summer school   £229
Knuston Hall *Irchester*
ARCA

9–14 August
2206 Hand coloured
     photographs   £AFD
Wye Valley Arts Centre *St. Briavel's,*
Glos
ARCA

9–15 August
2207 Christian Zen   £230
Ammerdown Centre *Radstock, Bath*

9–15 August
2208 Painting – foundation   £320
Dillington House *Ilminster*
ARCA

9–15 August
2209 Butterflies and moths   £243
Scottish Field Studies Association
Kindrogan Field Centre Pitlochry

9–15 August
2210 Bowls   £250/345
2211 Horse riding   £250/345
2212 Golf   £250/345
2213 Fitness, sport and
     adventure   £250/345
2214 Coast and country
     walks   £250/345
2215 Exploring the
     Quantocks   £250/345
2216 Hunkypunks and
     crocketed pinnacles   £250/345

111

9–15 August continued

2217	Somerset villages	£250/345
2218	Artists in Somerset	£250/345
2219	Arts a la carte	£250/345
2220	Private gardens	£250/345
2221	English country house	£250/345
2222	Antiques	£250/345
2223	Introduction to drawing and painting	£250/345
2224	Stained glass	£250/345
2225	Travels with your camera	£250/345
2226	Silverwork	£250/345
2227	Papier mache	£250/345
2228	Calligraphy	£250/345
2229	Art: working from the figure	£250/345
2230	Woodturning	£250/345
2231	Music and computers	£250/345
2232	Choral singing	£250/345
2233	Make piano your forte	£250/345
2234	Alexander Technique	£250/345
2235	Sense and nonsense in civilisation	£250/345
2236	Traveller's Spanish	£250/345
2237	Face reading	£250/345
2238	Computers (TSS Website)	£250/345
2239	Creative writing	£250/345
2240	Appearance matters	£250/345
2241	Speak with confidence	£250/345
2242	Design your own garden	£250/345
2243	Investment for beginners	£250/345

Taunton Summer School *Taunton*
All holidays open to family groups.

9–15 August

2244	Painting castles in watercolour	£169/397

Weobley Art Centre *Weobley, Herefordshire*
ARCA

9–16 August

2245	Summer art school	£333

Burton Manor College *South Wirral*
ARCA

9–16 August

2246	Painting and drawing – all media	£AFD

Wye Valley Arts Centre *St. Briavel's, Glos*
ARCA

10–11 August

2247	Tassels and cords	£50

Burton Manor College *South Wirral*
ARCA

10–13 August

2248	Yoga	£139
2249	Calligraphy	£139

Lancashire College *Chorley*
ARCA

10–13 August

2250	William Morris: designer extraordinary	£AFD

Maryland College *Woburn*
ARCA

10–14 August

2251	Block making in spartrie and other materials	£210
2252	Fashion fundamentals – illustration	£165
2253	Film, video and the 3rd wave	£385
2254	Introduction to illustration	£165
2255	Workshops in alternative life drawing	£210
2256	The fine print	£225
2257	Monoprint	£185
2258	Theatrical model-making	£255
2259	Using scrap	£210

Central Saint Martins College of Art and Design *London*
Price includes tuition only. Some courses also include material costs.

10–14 August

2260	Flatford family wildlife week	£AFD
2261	Life on the seashore	£142/180

Field Studies Council at Flatford Mill Field Centre *East Bergholt*

10–14 August
2262 Family wildlife discovery
week   £AFD
Field Studies Council at Juniper Hall
Field Centre *Dorking*

10–14 August
2263 Butterflies and moths   £175/225
Field Studies Council at Preston
Montford Field Centre *Shrewsbury*

10–14 August
2264 Porcelain restoration –
beginners   £235
Mowbray School of Porcelain
Restoration *Hatfield, Herts*

10–14 August
2265 Neo-Palladianism   £250
2266 The writer's craft   £250
2267 Roman Britain: its
archaeology explored   £250
Univ Cambridge *Madingley Hall*

10–15 August
2268 Gardens of Shropshire
and the Borderlands   £200/260
Field Studies Council at Preston
Montford Field Centre *Shrewsbury*

10–16 August
2269 Chinese brush painting   £230
2270 Improvers' painting   £230
2271 Yoga   £230
The Hill Residential Centre
Abergavenny
ARCA

10–16 August
2272 Machine knitting   £AFD
Urchfont Manor College *Devizes*
ARCA

11–12 August
2273 Life drawing   £AFD
Barn Crafts *Fincham, Norfolk*
Accommodation arranged on request.

11–30 August
2274 Super singing weeks for
children   £170
Sing for Pleasure *West Midlands*

12–14 August
2275 Golf – intermediate   £125
Knuston Hall *Irchester*
ARCA

12–19 August
2276 Landscape and seascape
painting   £187/247
2277 Natural history in the
Somerset hills   £208/268
2278 Exploring west
Somerset   £208/268
Field Studies Council at Nettlecombe
Court *Taunton, Somerset*

14–15 August
2279 Interior design on a
budget   £AFD
Barn Crafts *Fincham, Norfolk*
Accommodation arranged on request.

14–16 August
2280 Rural surprises   £175
Acorn Activities *Herefordshire,
Shropshire and Wales*

14–16 August
2281 Future world: the energy
question   £100/122
Field Studies Council at
Rhyd-y-creuau *Betws-y-coed*

14–16 August
2282 Mixed lace for all   £92
2283 Clothes making   £92
2284 Let's play jazz   £92
2285 The video camcorder   £92
Knuston Hall *Irchester*
ARCA

14–16 August
2286 Wildlife studies in
Bedfordshire   £99
Maryland College *Woburn*
ARCA

14–16 August
2287 Pen and ink techniques   £120
2288 Beethoven's piano
sonatas   £120
2289 Hidden voices   £120
Univ Cambridge *Madingley Hall*

113

14–16 August
2290 Cabinet making – part I   £AFD
2291 Caring for furniture   £AFD
2292 Gardening – the mixed
     border   £AFD
West Dean College *Chichester*
ARCA

14–17 August
2293 New directions in
     watercolour   £110/140
2294 Painting flowers and
     trees in garden settings £110/140
2295 Walking in Constable
     Country   £110/140
Field Studies Council at Flatford Mill
Field Centre *East Bergholt*

14–17 August
2296 Summer flowers of
     South Devon   £101/135
Field Studies Council at Slapton Ley
Field Centre *Kingsbridge, Devon*

14–21 August
2297 Country dance   £223/293
Belstead House *Ipswich*
ARCA

14–21 August
2298 Improve your painting:
     using oils and acrylics £221/280
Field Studies Council at Flatford Mill
Field Centre *East Bergholt*

14–21 August
2299 Painting late summer
     flowers and fruits in
     watercolour   £238/280
Field Studies Council at Juniper Hall
Field Centre *Dorking*

14–21 August
2300 Archaeology of the
     limestone Dales   £200/270
2301 Family activity week   £AFD
2302 Walking for inspiration £200/270
Field Studies Council at Malham Tarn
Field Centre *Settle, N Yorks*

14–21 August
2303 Creative writing   £195/260
2304 Natural history
     photography   £195/260
Field Studies Council at Slapton Ley
Field Centre *Kingsbridge, Devon*

14–21 August
2305 Landscape painting   £AFD
2306 Chinese brush painting
     summer school   £AFD
2307 One piece quilting   £AFD
The Old Rectory *Fittleworth*
ARCA

15–16 August
2308 Stained glass   £120
2309 Drystone walling   £80
2310 Drawing for the terrified   £96
2311 Silk painting   £100
Acorn Activities *Herefordshire,*
Shropshire and Wales

15–16 August
2312 Trance mediumship   £60
Mountain Hall *Queensbury*
Price includes tuition/lunches.
Accommodation/dinner, B/B £25 per
night.

15–18 August
2313 Summer flowers   £130
Scottish Field Studies Association
Kindrogan Field Centre Pitlochry

15–21 August
2314 Calligraphy   £250/300
2315 Impressionist
     landscapes   £250/300
Alston Hall Residential College
Preston
ARCA

15–21 August
2316 Clans and castles   £449
HF Holidays *Pitlochry*

15–21 August
2317 King Arthur: legend,
     history and literature   £430
2318 Music of the Celtic
     countries   £430
Summer Academy *Univ Wales,*
Aberystwyth

15–21 August continued
2319 Canterbury: portraits of a
    cathedral city £430
2320 From Romanesque to
    Gothic revival: the
    heritage of churches in
    Britain £460
Summer Academy *Univ Kent,*
Canterbury

15–21 August
2321 Town and country
    houses in Northumbria £430
2322 The Anglo-Scottish
    border £430
Summer Academy *Univ Durham*
2323 Sir Walter Scott:
    Scotland's saviour £460
2324 Scottish historic homes
    and gardens £460
Summer Academy *Univ Strathclyde,*
Glasgow
2325 Buildings, patrons and
    craftsmen in Tudor
    Yorkshire £430
2326 Plague, protest and
    parliament: England in
    the later Middle Ages £430
Summer Academy *Univ York*

15–21 August
2327 Film Festival £145
Univ Edinburgh *Edinburgh*

15–21 August
2328 38th Annual Esperanto
    School £175
Wedgwood Memorial College
Barlaston
ARCA

15–21 August
2329 Early music performance £AFD
West Dean College *Chichester*
ARCA

15–22 August
2330 Edinburgh Festival
    course (week 'A') £409*
Carberry *Musselburgh, Edinburgh*
includes all tickets.

15–22 August
2331 Ambling through a
    historic landscape £205/268
2332 Landscape painting in
    watercolours £205/268
2333 Linear walks £205/268
Field Studies Council at Blencathra
Field Centre *Threlkeld, Keswick*

15–22 August
2334 Discovery and adventure £AFD
2335 Discovery and
    adventure: young leaders £AFD
Field Studies Council at Castle Head
Field Centre *Grange-over-Sands*

15–22 August
2336 Pastel painting £AFD
2337 Lakeland walks £AFD
Higham Hall *Cockermouth*
ARCA

15–22 August
2338 Landscape painting £325
Painting in Pembrokeshire *St. David's*

15–22 August
2339 Sedges and rushes £294
2340 Beetles (terrestrial and
    aquatic) £294
Scottish Field Studies Association
Kindrogan Field Centre Pitlochry

15–22 August
2341 Primary teachers' week £270
2342 Youth singing week for
    14–18 year olds £180
Sing for Pleasure *Matlock, Derbys*

15–30 August
2343 Neuro-linguistic
    programming –
    practitioner intensive £920
Mountain Hall *Queensbury*
Price includes tuition/lunches.
Accommodation/dinner, B/B £25 per
night.

15 August–4 September
2344 The Edinburgh Festival
    (music, drama, The
    Fringe) £150/220*
Univ Edinburgh *Edinburgh*
per week, incl. theatre/concert
tickets.

16–21 August

2345	Mixed lace for all	£229
2346	Clothes making	£229
2347	Let's play jazz	£229

Knuston Hall *Irchester*
ARCA

16–21 August

2348	Woodturning	£AFD
2349	Watercolour painting	£AFD
2350	Harbours and seascapes in watercolour	£AFD

West Dean College *Chichester*
ARCA

16–21 August

2351	Beginners' basic drawing and painting	£AFD

Wye Valley Arts Centre *St. Briavel's, Glos*
ARCA

16–22 August

2352	Orchestra summer school	£230/270

Benslow Music Trust *Hitchin*
ARCA

16–22 August

2353	Painting animals	£320
2354	Rambling	£345
2355	Mosaics	£320

Dillington House *Ilminster*
ARCA

16–22 August

2356	Watercolours – beginners	£169/397

Weobley Art Centre *Weobley, Herefordshire*
ARCA

17–19 August

2357	Two queens in conflict	£AFD

Knuston Hall *Irchester*
ARCA

17–19 August

2358	Public voices	£120

Univ Cambridge *Madingley Hall*

17–21 August

2359	Silkscreen printing and the Mac	£525
2360	Still life drawing and painting	£150
2361	Design for shoes	£200
2362	Fashion fundamentals – design	£160
2363	Developing a personal approach to illustration	£165
2364	Life drawing with colour	£180
2365	Black and white printing	£225
2366	Ideas and techniques	£140
2367	Etching	£185
2368	Introduction to sculpture	£210
2369	Papier maché	£130
2370	Dance photography	£295
2371	Experimental jewellery	£180
2372	Graphic design	£155
2373	Exploration workshop in digital design	£525
2374	Mac as a fine art tool	£385

Central Saint Martins College of Art and Design *London*
Price includes tuition only. Some courses also include material costs.

17–21 August

2375	Cycling in Constable Country	£142/180
2376	Painting plants: late summer colours	£142/180
2377	Suffolk and Essex villages	£142/180

Field Studies Council at Flatford Mill Field Centre *East Bergholt*

17–21 August

2378	Grasses in flower	£192/220

Field Studies Council at Rhyd-y-creuau *Betws-y-coed*

17–21 August

2379	The Hallsands story: dramatic interpretations in words and music	£112/150

Field Studies Council at Slapton Ley Field Centre *Kingsbridge, Devon*

17–21 August

2380	The Normans in Britain	£214
2381	Rambling	£230

The Hill Residential Centre *Abergavenny*
ARCA

17–21 August
2382 Porcelain restoration –
     intermediate   £245
Mowbray School of Porcelain
Restoration *Hatfield, Herts*

17–21 August
2383 Children's course   £AFD
Scottish Field Studies Association
Kindrogan Field Centre Pitlochry

17–21 August
2384 Come behind the scenes   £250
Univ Cambridge *Madingley Hall*

17–21 August
2385 Calligraphy workshop   £AFD
Urchfont Manor College *Devizes*
ARCA

17–22 August
2386 Country houses of the
     West Country   £210
Ammerdown Centre *Radstock, Bath*

17 August–11 September
2387 Computers and graphic
     design   £1425
Central Saint Martins College of Art
and Design *London*
Price includes tuition only. Some
courses also include material costs.

18–19 August
2388 Enamelling pictures   £AFD
Barn Crafts *Fincham, Norfolk*
Accommodation arranged on request.

18–21 August
2389 Garden design   £AFD
West Dean College *Chichester*
ARCA

18–22 August
2390 Families   £AFD
Scottish Field Studies Association
Kindrogan Field Centre Pitlochry

18–25 August
2391 Spanish   £312
Lancashire College *Chorley*
ARCA

19–21 August
2392 Private voices   £120
Univ Cambridge *Madingley Hall*

19–26 August
2393 Landscape drawing and
     painting   £187/247
2394 Natural history on the
     Somerset coast   £208/268
2395 Woodland management
     and conservation   £208/268
Field Studies Council at Nettlecombe
Court *Taunton, Somerset*

21–22 August
2396 Life drawing   £AFD
Barn Crafts *Fincham, Norfolk*
Accommodation arranged on request.

21–23 August
2397 More Lancashire tales   £75/100
Alston Hall Residential College
Preston
ARCA

21–23 August
2398 Ballroom dancing   £98
Burton Manor College *South Wirral*
ARCA

21–23 August
2399 Rock climbing for
     women   £96/120
Field Studies Council at Castle Head
Field Centre *Grange-over-Sands*

21–23 August
2400 Composites: identifying
     the asteraceae   £89/115
Field Studies Council at Juniper Hall
Field Centre *Dorking*

21–23 August
2401 Look out for mammals:
     an identification
     workshop   £50/90
Field Studies Council at
Rhyd-y-creuau *Betws-y-coed*

21–23 August
2402 Writing your life story   £92
2403 Chinese brush painting   £92
Knuston Hall *Irchester*
ARCA

21–23 August
2404	Virgil's Aeneid Book 2	£120
2405	Spoken voices	£120
2406	English misericords and related church carvings	£120

Univ Cambridge *Madingley Hall*

21–23 August
2407	The island of Steepholm	£AFD
2408	The Amish people: culture and quilts	£AFD

Urchfont Manor College *Devizes*
ARCA

21–23 August
2409	Stencilling	£AFD

Wye Valley Arts Centre *St. Briavel's, Glos*
ARCA

21–24 August
2410	Drawing and sketching out of doors	£110/140
2411	Improve your watercolours	£110/140
2412	Walking in Constable Country	£110/140

Field Studies Council at Flatford Mill
Field Centre *East Bergholt*

21–24 August
2413	Practical drawing and painting – colour and the landscape	£180

Univ Cambridge *Madingley Hall*

21–28 August
2414	Improve your photography	£221/280

Field Studies Council at Flatford Mill
Field Centre *East Bergholt*

21–28 August
2415	Exploring the Settle to Carlisle Railway	£230/300
2416	Rambling through the Yorkshire Dales	£210/280

Field Studies Council at Malham Tarn
Field Centre *Settle, N Yorks*

21–28 August
2417	Natural history experience: Snowdonia and North Wales	£185/262
2418	Understanding conservation through Bryophytes	£235/312

Field Studies Council at
Rhyd-y-creuau *Betws-y-coed*

21–28 August
2419	Exploring along the Devon coast	£195/260
2420	Family naturalists: discovering Devon's wildlife	£AFD

Field Studies Council at Slapton Ley
Field Centre *Kingsbridge, Devon*

21–30 August
2421	Silversmithing	£AFD
2422	Silver engraving	£AFD

West Dean College *Chichester*
ARCA

22–23 August
2423	Tarot reading	£60

Mountain Hall *Queensbury*
Price includes tuition/lunches.
Accommodation/dinner, B/B £25 per night.

22–25 August
2424	Introduction to water plants	£136

Scottish Field Studies Association
Kindrogan Field Centre Pitlochry

22–28 August
2425	Prayer – theology and practice	£189
2426	Individually guided retreat	£189

Ammerdown Centre *Radstock, Bath*

22–28 August
2427	Fossil hunting	£399

HF Holidays *Selworthy*
2428	Literary Lakeland	£399

HF Holidays *Derwentwater*
2429	Landscape photography	£374
2430	Singing for beginners	£334

HF Holidays *Conwy*
2431	Monteverdi to Mozart	£354

HF Holidays *Coniston Water*

22–28 August continued

2432 Railways and sightseeing
in the South West £444
HF Holidays *Lyme Regis*

22–28 August

2433 Celtic landscapes £430
2434 Wild plants of West
Wales £430
Summer Academy *Univ Wales,
Aberystwyth*
2435 Evolution of a Kent
village: architecture and
social change £430
2436 The Victorian novel £395
Summer Academy *Univ Kent,
Canterbury*
2437 The medieval church –
architecture and imagery £430
2438 Yorkshire writers: people
and places £430
Summer Academy *Univ York*

22–28 August

2439 8th Classical Guitar
Festival of Great Britain £AFD
West Dean College *Chichester
ARCA*

22–29 August

2440 Wind plus summer
school £259/299
Benslow Music Trust *Hitchin
ARCA*

22–29 August

2441 Edinburgh Festival (week
'B') £409*
Carberry *Musselburgh, Edinburgh*
includes all tickets.

22–29 August

2442 Butterflies and moths £205/268
2443 Lake District life and
tradition £205/268
2444 Lakeland's quieter
corners £205/268
2445 Photographing Lakeland
in summer £205/268
Field Studies Council at Blencathra
Field Centre *Threlkeld, Keswick*

22–29 August

2446 Highland walks £283
2447 Fungi week £294
2448 Scotland's geological
heritage £299
Scottish Field Studies Association
Kindrogan Field Centre Pitlochry

22–30 August

2449 Summer school for
singers, teachers and
conductors £270
Sing for Pleasure *Matlock, Derbys*

22–30 August

2450 Summer school for
string players, solo
singers, choirs, string
orchestra etc. £AFD
Summer Music *Ardingly College
Sussex*

22 August–4 September

2451 New writing in English
(poetry/short story) £115/215
Univ Edinburgh *Edinburgh*

23–26 August

2452 Steam and water £200
2453 C18th England £175
2454 Birds, bugs, blooms and
butterflies £299
Dillington House *Ilminster
ARCA*

23–28 August

2455 Lacemaking with bobbin
or needle £200/250
Alston Hall Residential College
*Preston
ARCA*

23–28 August

2456 Chinese brush painting £229
Knuston Hall *Irchester
ARCA*

23–29 August

2457 Discovery and adventure
for adults £233/299
Field Studies Council at Castle Head
Field Centre *Grange-over-Sands*

23–29 August
2458 Further pen and ink with
  watercolour £169/397
Weobley Art Centre *Weobley,*
Herefordshire
ARCA

23–30 August
2459 Clay sculpture £AFD
Wye Valley Arts Centre *St. Briavel's,*
Glos
ARCA

24–25 August
2460 Decorative interiors and
  paint effects £100
Acorn Activities *Herefordshire,*
Shropshire and Wales

24–28 August
2461 Embroidery £190
2462 Writers' workshop £190
Burton Manor College *South Wirral*
ARCA

24–28 August
2463 Fashion fundamentals –
  portfolio presentation £155
2464 Life drawing in
  printmaking £195
2465 Sculpture workshop £160
2466 Colour mixing workshop £55
2467 Papermaking £130
2468 Typography £195
2469 Image of the feminine
  self £165
2470 Portfolio sketchbook £150
2471 Premiere and after
  effects for beginners £550
2472 Introduction to freehand
  and illustrator £525
2473 Drawing course £135
Central Saint Martins College of Art
and Design *London*
Price includes tuition only. Some
courses also include material costs.

24–28 August
2474 Birdwatching and bird
  migration in early
  autumn £142/180
2475 Improve your painting:
  skies, light and
  atmosphere £142/180
2476 Watercolour – absolute
  beginners £142/180
Field Studies Council at Flatford Mill
Field Centre *East Bergholt*

24–28 August
2477 Family wildlife discovery
  week £AFD
Field Studies Council at Juniper Hall
Field Centre *Dorking*

24–28 August
2478 An introduction to NVC:
  swamps, fens and
  mires £175/225
2479 Water plants: training for
  professionals £190/295
Field Studies Council at Preston
Montford Field Centre *Shrewsbury*

24–28 August
2480 Ferns: identification,
  biology and implications
  for management £176/220
Field Studies Council at
Rhyd-y-creuau *Betws-y-coed*

24–28 August
2481 Open University £AFD
Lancashire College *Chorley*
ARCA

24–28 August
2482 Porcelain restoration –
  advanced £255
Mowbray School of Porcelain
Restoration *Hatfield, Herts*

24–28 August
2483 Reading Latin week £120/250
2484 Practical drawing and
  painting – landscape and
  weather and time of day £250
2485 Ways of putting it £250
2486 French week £250
Univ Cambridge *Madingley Hall*

24–28 August
2487 Bobbin lacemaking £AFD
2488 Creative tapestry
weaving £AFD
2489 Painting landscapes £AFD
Urchfont Manor College *Devizes*
ARC:A

25–26 August
2490 Longbow making £AFD
Barn Crafts *Fincham, Norfolk*
Accommodation arranged on request.

26–30 August
2491 Bat ecology £140/180
Field Studies Council at Orielton Field
Centre *Pembroke*

26 August–2 September
2492 Walking the
Pembrokeshire coast
path £209/268
Field Studies Council at Dale Fort
Field Centre *Haverfordwest*

26 August–2 September
2493 Out and about again £208/268
Field Studies Council at Nettlecombe
Court *Taunton, Somerset*

26 August–2 September
2494 Botanical illustration £200/260
2495 Spiders and their
identification £200/260
2496 Trees and their
identification £200/260
Field Studies Council at Orielton Field
Centre *Pembroke*

27–30 August
2497 Alexander Technique £157
Knuston Hall *Irchester*
ARCA

28–29 August
2498 Life drawing £AFD
Barn Crafts *Fincham, Norfolk*
Accommodation arranged on request.

28–30 August
2499 Wildlife sound recording £75/105
Field Studies Council at Preston
Montford Field Centre *Shrewsbury*

28–30 August
2500 Calligraphy £92
2501 Painting including
Impressionism £92
Knuston Hall *Irchester*
ARCA

28–30 August
2502 Early Christian art and
architecture £120
2503 Playing Bach on the
organ £120
2504 Advanced botanical
illustration £120
Univ Cambridge *Madingley Hall*

28–31 August
2505 Modelling in clay £115/160
Alston Hall Residential College
Preston
ARCA

28–31 August
2506 Harvestman spiders:
recognition and ecology £111/142
Field Studies Council at Dale Fort
Field Centre *Haverfordwest*

28–31 August
2507 Basic botany for
gardeners £100/135
Field Studies Council at Preston
Montford Field Centre *Shrewsbury*

28–31 August
2508 Gardens around York £AFD
Univ Nottingham *York*

28 August–1 September
2509 Diving the Skomer
Marine Reserve and
Pembrokeshire Islands £160/205
Field Studies Council at Dale Fort
Field Centre *Haverfordwest*

28 August–4 September
2510 Birds and bird migration £238/280
2511 Insect photography £218/275
2512 Landscape painting and
drawing £238/280
Field Studies Council at Juniper Hall
Field Centre *Dorking*

28 August–4 September
2513 A naturalist in
     Shropshire   £140/245
2514 Watercolours   £190/255
2515 Exploring Offa's Dyke £140/245
Field Studies Council at Preston
Montford Field Centre *Shrewsbury*

29 August–4 September
2516 Parchment craft   £294
HF Holidays *Loch Leven*
2517 Wildlife woodcarving   £469
2518 Drawing and walking   £439
HF Holidays *Abingworth*
2519 Opera   £359
HF Holidays *Freshwater Bay*
2520 Waterways of Yorkshire £464
HF Holidays *Malhamdale*

29 August–5 September
2521 Painting and prayer
     retreat   £AFD
Carberry *Musselburgh, Edinburgh*

29 August–5 September
2522 High peaks   £205/268
2523 Introduction to ferns £222/285
2524 Linear waiks   £205/268
2525 Steaming round the
     Lakes   £229/292
Field Studies Council at Blencathra
Field Centre *Threlkeld, Keswick*

29 August–5 September
2526 Mosses and liverworts £294
2527 Trees and woodland
     management   £294
Scottish Field Studies Association
Kindrogan Field Centre Pitlochry

30 August–3 September
2528 Dyeing, discharge and
     devoree on silk, mixed
     fabric and velvet   £AFD
West Dean College *Chichester*
ARCA

30 August–4 September
2529 Botanical illustration –
     beginners   £168/215
Field Studies Council at Flatford Mill
Field Centre *East Bergholt*

30 August–4 September
2530 Calligraphy   £229
2531 Painting including
     Impressionism   £229
Knuston Hall *Irchester*
ARCA

30 August–4 September
2532 Silversmithing and
     jewellery   £AFD
2533 Painting the Sussex
     landscape and traditional
     buildings in watercolour £AFD
West Dean College *Chichester*
ARCA

30 August–4 September
2534 Watercolour painting £AFD
Wye Valley Arts Centre *St. Briavels,
Glos*
ARCA

30 August–5 September
2535 Pottery with other
     activities   £395
Acorn Activities *Herefordshire,
Shropshire and Wales*

30 August–5 September
2536 Watercolour sketchbook £169/397
Weobley Art Centre *Weobley,
Herefordshire*
ARCA

30 August–6 September
2537 Landscape painting in
     the Yorkshire Dales £200/270
Field Studies Council at Malham Tarn
Field Centre *Settle, N Yorks*

31 August–4 September
2538 Drawing and painting £150/200
2539 Machine knitting   £150/200
Alston Hall Residential College
Preston
ARCA

31 August–5 September
2540 London Brass summer
     school   £225/265
Benslow Music Trust *Hitchin*
ARCA

■   ■   ■   ■

September 1998

☐   ☐   ☐   ☐

September
2541 Intermediate word
      processing   £AFD
2542 Intermediate
      spreadsheets   £AFD
2543 Study skills in higher
      education   £AFD
Univ Lancaster Summer School
Lancaster

3 days tba
2544 Country houses of South
      Wales and The Marches   £AFD
Univ Liverpool *South Wales*

1–2 September
2545 Acrylics   £AFD
Barn Crafts *Fincham, Norfolk*
Accommodation arranged on request.

1–4 September
2546 Egyptology   £143
Burton Manor College *South Wirral*
ARCA

1–4 September
2547 Fashion fundamentals –
      pattern cutting   £275
2548 Video animation
      workshop   £280
2549 Colour in jewellery   £250
2550 Life drawing   £150
2551 Figure drawing into
      painting   £185
2552 Watercolour painting   £165
2553 Photography portfolio   £225
2554 Silk-screen printing   £185
2555 Textile portfolio course £140
2556 Drawing into painting   £155
2557 Experiments in
      scriptwriting for narrative
      film   £175
2558 Eranded packaging
      design   £250
2559 Director for beginners   £440

1–4 September continued
2560 Playtime   £150
2561 Digital video on the
      desktop   £440
2562 Evening photography –
      portraiture   £180
**Central Saint Martins College of Art
and Design** *London*
*Price includes tuition only. Some
courses also include material costs.*

1–4 September
2563 Introducing lichens   £136
Scottish Field Studies Association
Kindrogan Field Centre Pitlochry

1–30 September
2564 Bird watching   £45*
2565 Flower arranging   £50*
2566 Drawing, oil painting and
      watercolours   £40*
2567 Basket making with cane   £50*
2568 Rush seating   £45*
2569 Cane seating   £45*
2570 Needlecraft   £40*
2571 Pottery (any Thursday)   £50
2572 Rural surprises (any
      weekend: minimum of 6
      people)   £175
2573 Woodwork (any
      consecutive 3 days
      except Sunday)   £165
2574 Furniture restoration (any
      consecutive 3 days
      except Sunday)   £165
2575 Landscape painting (any
      Sunday/Friday)   £375
2576 Chair making (any
      Monday/Friday:
      minimum of 2 people)   £250
2577 Bookbinding (any
      Monday/Friday:
      minimum of 2 people)   £250
Acorn Activities *Herefordshire,
Shropshire and Wales*
**Per day. Bookings can be made for
any number of days.*

2–4 September
2578 Still life painting   £98
Burton Manor College *South Wirral*
ARCA

2–9 September
2579 Lichens   £200/260
Field Studies Council at Orielton Field
Centre *Pembroke*

3–5 September
2580 Bridge   £109
Maryland College *Woburn*
ARCA

3–6 September
2581 Microscopy   £112/142
Belstead House *Ipswich*
ARCA

3–6 September
2582 Along the coastal
          footpath   £108/133
Field Studies Council at Nettlecombe
Court *Taunton, Somerset*

3–7 September
2583 An introduction to
          botanical illustration   £144/184
Field Studies Council at Dale Fort
Field Centre *Haverfordwest*

4–5 September
2584 Sculpture   £AFD
Barn Crafts *Fincham, Norfolk*
Accommodation arranged on request.

4–6 September
2585 Drawing for the terrified
          II   £75/100
2586 Hardanger embroidery   £75/100
Alston Hall Residential College
Preston
ARCA

4–6 September
2587 Aspects of Georgian art
          and design   £78/98
Belstead House *Ipswich*
ARCA

4–6 September
2588 Botanical painting   £98
Burton Manor College *South Wirral*
ARCA

4–6 September
2589 Have a go at canoeing   £96/120
Field Studies Council at Castle Head
Field Centre *Grange-over-Sands*

4–6 September
2590 Freshwater algae   £82/105
2591 Drawing, sketching and
          watercolour – improvers   £82/105
Field Studies Council at
Flatford Mill Field Centre *East*
Bergholt

4–6 September
2592 Bats   £78/102
2593 Fungus weekend I   £86/111
Field Studies Council at Juniper Hall
Field Centre *Dorking*

4–6 September
2594 Dormice   £75/105
2595 In search of Cadfael's
          landscape   £75/105
2596 Sketching and painting
          techniques for landscape   £75/105
2597 Water and wetlands   £75/105
Field Studies Council at Preston
Montford Field Centre *Shrewsbury*

4–6 September
2598 An introduction to
          chamber music   £AFD
2599 The malt whiskeys of
          Scotland   £92
2600 Essential electric guitar   £92
Knuston Hall *Irchester*
ARCA

4–6 September
2601 The interpretation and
          enjoyment of English
          medieval churches   £129
Univ Birmingham *Ludlow, Shropshire*

4–6 September
2602 Charles Rennie
          Mackintosh: ambivalent
          Modernist   £120
2603 Autumn birds   £120
2604 East Anglia in the 2nd
          Civil War   £120
2605 Railway heritage   £120
Univ Cambridge *Madingley Hall*

4–6 September
2606 Dormice and otters   £AFD
Univ Nottingham *Axbridge*
2607 Medieval Cambridge   £AFD
Univ Nottingham *Lucy Cavendish College Cambridge*
2608 Introduction to chamber
        music   £AFD
Univ Nottingham *Knuston Hall*
2609 Historic York
Univ Nottingham *Univ Coll of Ripon & York St John, York*

4–6 September
2610 Classic British movies:
        Ealing   £AFD
2611 Making teddy bears   £AFD
Urchfont Manor College *Devizes*
ARCA

4–6 September
2612 Portrait painting and
        drawing   £AFD
2613 Decorative chainmaking
        and linking systems   £AFD
West Dean College *Chichester*
ARCA

4–6 September
2614 Botanical painting and
        drawing   £AFD
Wye Valley Arts Centre *St. Briavels, Glos*
ARCA

4–8 September
2615 Marbling on paper   £AFD
West Dean College *Chichester*
ARCA

4–9 September
2616 Autumn birds of
        Snowdonia and the
        North Wales coast   £152/207
Field Studies Council at
Rhyd-y-creuau *Betws-y-coed*

4–11 September
2617 Trees and woodlands in
        the British countryside   £249/325
Field Studies Council at Flatford Mill
Field Centre *East Bergholt*

4–11 September
2618 Working with a flora   £216/275
Field Studies Council at Juniper Hall
Field Centre *Dorking*

4–11 September
2619 Applique, collage and
        stitch   £AFD
2620 Ivor and Noel – a week
        for singers   £AFD
2621 Painting in water based
        media   £AFD
The Old Rectory *Fittleworth*
ARCA

4–11 September
2622 Portrait modelling from
        life   £AFD
West Dean College *Chichester*
ARCA

4–11 September
2623 Papermaking   £AFD
Wye Valley Arts Centre *St. Briavels, Glos*
ARCA

5–6 September
2624 Woodturning   £100
2625 Pottery   £100
Acorn Activities *Herefordshire, Shropshire and Wales*

5–6 September
2626 Crystal energies   £60
Mountain Hall *Queensbury*
Price includes tuition/lunches. Accommodation/dinner, B/B £25 per night.

5–7 September
2627 Introduction to geology   £80/104
2628 Stone circles   £80/104
Field Studies Council at Blencathra
Field Centre *Threlkeld, Keswick*

5–8 September
2629 Yoga   £204
HF Holidays *Conwy*

5–8 September
2630 Working with willow   £136
Scottish Field Studies Association
Kindrogan Field Centre Pitlochry

5–11 September
2631 Creative writing £319
HF Holidays *Lyme Regis*
2632 Scrabble, walking and
sight-seeing (for all
levels) £339
HF Holidays *Freshwater Bay*

5–11 September
2633 Understanding scenery £395
Summer Academy *Univ Wales,
Swansea*

5–12 September
2634 Landscape photography £222/285
2635 Mosses and liverworts £222/285
Field Studies Council at Blencathra
Field Centre *Threlkeld, Keswick*

5–12 September
2636 A people in their
landscape (Highland
history) £294
2637 Eating fungi £294
Scottish Field Studies Association
Kindrogan Field Centre Pitlochry

6–11 September
2638 Fabric collage – machine
embroidery £200/250
Alston Hall Residential College
Preston
ARCA

6–11 September
2639 Mountain leader
assessment £228/270
Field Studies Council at
Rhyd-y-creuau *Betws-y-coed*

6–11 September
2640 Landscape painting £385
Painting in Pembrokeshire *St. Davids*

6–11 September
2641 Migrating birds £AFD
Univ Nottingham *Gibraltar Point Field
Station*

6–11 September
2642 Printmaking workshop £AFD
2643 Drawing and painting
landscape £AFD
West Dean College *Chichester*
ARCA

6–11 September
2644 Chinese brush painting £AFD
Wye Valley Arts Centre *St. Briavels,
Glos*
ARCA

6–12 September
2645 Pottery with other
activities £395
Acorn Activities *Herefordshire,
Shropshire and Wales*

6–12 September
2646 Watercolour week £169/397
Weobley Art Centre *Weobley,
Herefordshire*
ARCA

7–11 September
2647 Creative painting £180
2648 Fashion fundamentals –
sewing £275
2649 Publishing on the
Internet £550
2650 Block printing £185
2651 Colour in design £150
Central Saint Martins College of Art
and Design *London*
*Price includes tuition only. Some
courses also include material costs.*

7–11 September
2652 Records and residencies £250
Univ Cambridge *Madingley Hall*

7–12 September
2653 Get talking in French £200
Meirionnydd Languages
Trawsfynydd, North Wales

8–9 September
2654 Watercolour painting on
location £AFD
Barn Crafts *Fincham, Norfolk*
Accommodation arranged on request.

8–11 September
2655 Fungi for intermediates £130
Scottish Field Studies Association
Kindrogan Field Centre Pitlochry

9–11 September
2656 Churches in Rutland £AFD
Univ Nottingham *Rutland*

10–13 September
2657 Stained glass workshop   £143
Burton Manor College *South Wirral*
ARCA

11–12 September
2658 Interior design on a
    budget   £AFD
Barn Crafts *Fincham, Norfolk*
Accommodation arranged on request.

11–13 September
2659 Painting weekend   £75/100
2660 Enamelling   £75/100
Alston Hall Residential College
Preston
ARCA

11–13 September
2661 Woodcarving   £98
Burton Manor College *South Wirral*
ARCA

11–13 September
2662 Walking three Suffolk
    estuaries   £82/105
2663 Watercolour – absolute
    beginners   £82/105
**Field Studies Council at Flatford Mill
Field Centre** *East Bergholt*

11–13 September
2664 Fungus weekend II   £86/111
**Field Studies Council at Juniper Hall
Field Centre** *Dorking*

11–13 September
2665 Farming and the
    environment   £75/105
2666 Historic townscapes   £75/105
2667 Vintage transport   £85/110
**Field Studies Council at Preston
Montford Field Centre** *Shrewsbury*

11–13 September
2668 Astronomy   £AFD
Horncastle College *Horncastle*
ARCA

11–13 September
2669 Reflexology   £92
2670 Tai-Chi   £92
2671 Aromatherapy   £92
2672 Reiki healing   £92
Knuston Hall *Irchester*
ARCA

11–13 September
2673 Basic china mending   £135
**Mowbray School of Porcelain
Restoration** *Hatfield, Herts*

11–13 September
2674 Autumn birds   £AFD
2675 Natural watercolours   £AFD
2676 John Bull's other island:
    Ireland 1798–1922   £AFD
2677 Music appreciation   £AFD
The Old Rectory *Fittleworth*
ARCA

11–13 September
2678 Alexander Technique   £AFD
2679 Calligraphy   £AFD
2680 Video filming   £AFD
2681 Lacemaking   £AFD
Pendrell Hall College *Staffs*
ARCA

11–13 September
2682 Ferns   £91
2683 Introduction to fungi   £91
2684 Countryside/environmental
    law   £85
Scottish Field Studies Association
Kindrogan Field Centre Pitlochry

11–13 September
2685 Plant hunters   £120
2686 Trilobite evolution and
    Ordovician environments
    in central Wales   £AFD
2687 Antiques: topic tbc   £120
Univ Cambridge *Madingley Hall*

11–13 September
2688 Making the most of your
    greenhouse   £AFD
2689 Caring for furniture   £AFD
2690 Woodcarving   £AFD
2691 Oil painting   £AFD
West Dean College *Chichester*
ARCA

11–13 September
2692 Tai Chi   £AFD
Wye Valley Arts Centre *St. Briavels, Glos*
ARCA

11–14 September
2693 Singing for pleasure   £98
2694 The life and works of
      Leos Janacek   £98
Burton Manor College *South Wirral*
ARCA

11–14 September
2695 Cuttle fish casting and
      etching on metal as
      surface decoration for
      jewellery making   £AFD
West Dean College *Chichester*
ARCA

11–18 September
2696 Natural history of south
      Lakeland   £198/268
Field Studies Council at Castle Head
Field Centre *Grange-over-Sands*

11–18 September
2697 Abstract painting   £AFD
Wye Valley Arts Centre *St. Briavels, Glos*
ARCA

12–13 September
2698 Basket making with
      English willow   £100
Acorn Activities *Herefordshire, Shropshire and Wales*

12–18 September
2699 Literary quest in
      Yorkshire   £449
2700 Steam traction in
      Yorkshire   £499
HF Holidays *Whitby*
2701 Theatre appreciation   £449
2702 Clans and castles   £449
HF Holidays *Pitlochry*
2703 Gaelic heritage   £384
HF Holidays *Loch Leven*
2704 Landscape photography   £339
HF Holidays *Arran*
2705 Landscape photography   £376
HF Holidays *Thurlestone Sands*

13–18 September
2706 Landscape painting   £385
Painting in Pembrokeshire *St. Davids*

13–18 September
2707 Stained glass and glass
      painting   £AFD
2708 Botanical illustration   £AFD
2709 Cabinet making – part 2   £AFD
2710 Writing and illustrating
      books for young readers   £AFD
2711 Decorative painting on
      furniture   £AFD
West Dean College *Chichester*
ARCA

13–19 September
2712 Pottery with other
      activities   £395
Acorn Activities *Herefordshire, Shropshire and Wales*

13–19 September
2713 Flowers in the studio   £169/397
Weobley Art Centre *Weobley, Herefordshire*
ARCA

13–20 September
2714 Creative writing   £AFD
Wye Valley Arts Centre *St. Briavels, Glos*
ARCA

14–17 September
2715 The bead workshop   £AFD
West Dean College *Chichester*
ARCA

15–16 September
2716 Life drawing   £AFD
Barn Crafts *Fincham, Norfolk*
Accommodation arranged on request.

17–20 September
2717 Nettlecombe fungus
      foray   £108/133
Field Studies Council at Nettlecombe
Court *Taunton, Somerset*

18–19 September
2718 Acrylics   £AFD
Barn Crafts *Fincham, Norfolk*
Accommodation arranged on request.

133

18–20 September
2719 Choral singing   £75/100
2720 Goldsmithing   £75/100
Alston Hall Residential College
Preston
ARCA

18–20 September
2721 Dartington Hall Violin
        Conference   £AFD
Dartington Hall *Totnes, Devon*

18–20 September
2722 The green man: myth
        and symbolism   £80/104
Field Studies Council at Castle Head
Field Centre *Grange-over-Sands*

18–20 September
2723 East Anglian steam
        railways   £82/105
2724 Making your camera
        work for you   £82/105
2725 Improve your
        watercolours   £82/105
Field Studies Council at Flatford Mill
Field Centre *East Bergholt*

18–20 September
2726 Spiders in autumn   £78/102
Field Studies Council at Juniper Hall
Field Centre *Dorking*

18–20 September
2727 C & G lace – I and II   £83
2728 The Knights Templar   £AFD
2729 Aspects of pastel   £AFD
Knuston Hall *Irchester*
ARCA

18–20 September
2730 John Ruskin – a study of
        his life and work   £99
Maryland College *Woburn*
ARCA

18–20 September
2731 Painting: wet in wet   £AFD
2732 Make a traditional
        collectors teddy bear   £AFD
2733 Woodland toadstools   £AFD
The Old Rectory *Fittleworth*
ARCA

18–20 September
2734 Singing weekend   £95
Sing for Pleasure *Harrogate*

18–20 September
2735 The altarpiece in the
        Italian Renaissance   £120
2736 Luke – historian/
        theologian   £120
Univ Cambridge *Madingley Hall*

18–20 September
2737 The novels of Joseph
        Conrad   £AFD
2738 Emotions – friend or foe   £AFD
2739 Victorian art and life   £AFD
2740 The grey queens –
        Elizabeth Woodville and
        Lady Jane Grey   £AFD
2741 Computing – surfing the
        Internet   £AFD
2742 Introduction to
        contemporary music   £AFD
2743 Creative couples in art   £AFD
Univ Nottingham *Nottingham*

18–20 September
2744 Honiton lacemaking   £AFD
2745 Cords and tassels   £AFD
Urchfont Manor College *Devizes*
ARCA

18–20 September
2746 Calligraphy   £AFD
2747 Batik on silk   £AFD
2748 Life drawing   £AFD
2749 The Faust legend in
        music   £AFD
2750 Ceramic decoration
        using slip and majolica   £AFD
2751 Creative watercolour for
        beginners   £AFD
2752 Lettercarving in stone
        and slate   £AFD
West Dean College *Chichester*
ARCA

18–20 September
2753 Beginners' basic drawing
        and painting   £AFD
Wye Valley Arts Centre *St. Briavels,
Glos*
ARCA

WYE VALLEY ARTS CENTRE, GLOUCESTERSHIRE

18–25 September
2754 Observing and recording
plant structure　　　£233/275
Field Studies Council at Juniper Hall
Field Centre *Dorking*

19–20 September
2755 Have you lived before?
Exploring your past lives　　£60
Mountain Hall *Queensbury*
Price includes tuition/lunches.
Accommodation/dinner, B/B £25 per
night.

19–21 September
2756 Prehistoric
Caernarfonshire　　　£AFD
Univ Liverpool *Bangor*

19–22 September
2757 British plant
communities　　　£145
Field Studies Council at Epping Forest
Field Centre *Loughton, Essex*

19–25 September
2758 North Wales Music
Festival　　　£344
HF Holidays *Conwy*
2759 Daphne Du Maurier's
Cornwall　　　£399
HF Holidays *St Ives*

19–25 September
2760 T'ai Chi and walking　　£334
HF Holidays *Isle of Arran*

20–24 September
2761 Drawing and painting on
silk　　　£AFD
West Dean College *Chichester*
ARCA

20–25 September
2762 Geology of the Lake
District　　　£AFD
Higham Hall *Cockermouth*
ARCA

20–25 September
2763 Cane and rush seating,
willow and rush basketry　£AFD
2764 Fabric murals and
wallhangings　　　£AFD
2765 Gilding part 1　　　£AFD
West Dean College *Chichester*
ARCA

20–25 September
2766 Watercolour painting　　£AFD
Wye Valley Arts Centre *St. Briavels,*
Glos
ARCA

20–26 September
2767 Pots and flowers in
watercolour　　£169/397
Weobley Art Centre *Weobley,*
Herefordshire
ARCA

20–27 September
2768 Landscapes (all media)　£AFD
Higham Hall *Cockermouth*
ARCA

21–23 September
2769 Alexander Technique
workshop　　£80/110
Alston Hall Residential College
Preston
ARCA

21–25 September
2770 Autumn holiday for the
young at heart 50+　　£110
Ammerdown Centre *Radstock, Bath*

21–25 September
2771 Acrylic painting　　　£215
2772 Somerset Levels　　　£250
2773 Parchment craft　　　£210
Dillington House *Ilminster*
ARCA

21–25 September
2774 Porcelain restoration –
beginners　　　£235
Mowbray School of Porcelain
Restoration *Hatfield, Herts*

21–25 September
2775 Making and mending
      books   £AFD
2776 Romance of the theatre   £AFD
2777 Painting course   £AFD
The Old Rectory *Fittleworth*
ARCA

22–23 September
2778 Sculpture   £AFD
Barn Crafts *Fincham, Norfolk*
Accommodation arranged on request.

24–27 September
2779 Fungus fun   £108/133
Field Studies Council at Nettlecombe
Court *Taunton, Somerset*

25–26 September
2780 Watercolour painting on
      location   £AFD
Barn Crafts *Fincham, Norfolk*
Accommodation arranged on request.

25–27 September
2781 Chinese brush painting
      (int/advanced)   £75/100
2782 First World War battles £75/100
2783 Honiton lacemaking   £75/100
Alston Hall Residential College
Preston
ARCA

25–27 September
2784 Autumn woodlands   £80/104
2785 Lakeland through the
      lens   £80/104
2786 Wild cookery   £90/114
Field Studies Council at Blencathra
Field Centre *Threlkeld, Keswick*

25–27 September
2787 Painting plants: early
      autumn colours   £82/105
2788 Suffolk's medieval
      houses   £82/105
2789 Watercolour for near
      beginners   £82/105
Field Studies Council at Flatford Mill
Field Centre *East Bergholt*

25–27 September
2790 Deadly and delightful   £AFD
Higham Hall *Cockermouth*
ARCA

25–27 September
2791 Bridge for improvers   £92
2792 Writing and illustrating
      books for young people   £92
2793 Skirts and waistcoats   £92
2794 The Tresham Trail   £AFD
Knuston Hall *Irchester*
ARCA

25–27 September
2795 T'ai Chi Chuan   £AFD
2796 Painting course   £AFD
The Old Rectory *Fittleworth*
ARCA

25–27 September
2797 Chinese brush painting   £AFD
Pendrell Hall College *Staffs*
ARCA

25–27 September
2798 Guitar orchestra   £AFD
2799 Putting over a song   £AFD
Summer Music *Hassocks, Sussex*

25–27 September
2800 Reading Classical Greek £120
2801 Emily Dickinson   £120
2802 English hymns and
      hymnwriters   £120
2803 Woods of East Anglia   £120
Univ Cambridge *Madingley Hall*

25–27 September
2804 London's River Police
      1798–1998   £AFD
Univ Nottingham *London*

25–27 September
2805 The 3 ages of opera part
      1   £AFD
Urchfont Manor College *Devizes*
ARCA

25–27 September
2806   Cabinet making – part 1   £AFD
2807   Relief stone carving   £AFD
2808   Getting started with
       watercolour   £AFD
2809   Dreams and fairy tales –
       a painting course   £AFD
2810   Colour photography   £AFD
2811   Calligraphy: italic and
       capitals   £AFD
West Dean College *Chichester*
ARCA

25–27 September
2812   Quiltmaking: make a
       quilt in a weekend   £AFD
2813   Gregorian chant study   £AFD
Wye Valley Arts Centre *St. Briavels,*
Glos
ARCA

25–28 September
2814   Small mammals:
       recognition and ecology £111/142
Field Studies Council at Dale Fort
Field Centre *Haverfordwest*

25–28 September
2815   Useful plants   £101/135
Field Studies Council at Slapton Ley
Field Centre *Kingsbridge, Devon*

25–28 September
2816   Basic blacksmithing   £AFD
West Dean College *Chichester*
ARCA

26–27 September
2817   Silversmithing and
       jewellery   £120
Acorn Activities *Herefordshire,*
Shropshire and Wales

26–27 September
2818   Partner massage   £60
Mountain Hall *Queensbury*
Price includes tuition/lunches.
Accommodation/dinner, B/B £25 per
night.

26–29 September
2819   Reflexology   £174
HF Holidays *Thurlestone Sands*

26 September–2 October
2820   Birdwatching in
       Snowdonia and the
       Conwy estuary   £349
HF Holidays *Conwy*
2821   Arran's autumn wildlife   £349
HF Holidays *Isle of Arran*
2822   Historic houses of
       Derbyshire   £379
HF Holidays *Dovedale*

27 September–1 October
2823   Getting the best from
       your camera   £AFD
West Dean College *Chichester*
ARCA

27 September–2 October
2824   Wet into wet
       watercolour   £AFD
2825   More secret Lakeland
       walks   £AFD
Higham Hall *Cockermouth*
ARCA

27 September–2 October
2826   Mouldmaking and
       casting for sculpture   £AFD
2827   Oil painting – the
       painterly approach   £AFD
West Dean College *Chichester*
ARCA

27 September–2 October
2828   Batik and fabric painting   £AFD
Wye Valley Arts Centre *St. Briavels,*
Glos
ARCA

27 September–3 October
2829   Watercolour week   £169/397
Weobley Art Centre *Weobley,*
Herefordshire
ARCA

27 September–4 October
2830   Interiors and still-life
       painting – all media   £AFD
Wye Valley Arts Centre *St. Briavels,*
Glos
ARCA

28 September–2 October
2831 Porcelain restoration –
  intermediate   £245
Mowbray School of Porcelain
Restoration *Hatfield, Herts*

28 September–4 October
2832 Cabinet making – part 3   £AFD
West Dean College *Chichester
ARCA*

29–30 September
2833 Embroidery without kits   £AFD
Barn Crafts *Fincham, Norfolk*
Accommodation arranged on request.

30 September–2 October
2834 Colour reflexology   £129
HF Holidays *Thurlestone Sands*

30 September–2 October
2835 Cambridge libraries   £120
Univ Cambridge *Madingley Hall*

THE UNIVERSITY
OF BIRMINGHAM

School of Continuing Studies

Study Breaks in Britain and Abroad

The School of Continuing Studies at the University of Birmingham offers a wide range of study breaks in Britain and abroad. In 1998 these will include: 'Discovering Derbyshire's Gardens', 'The Interpretation and Enjoyment of English Medieval Churches', 'Burne-Jones and the Pre-Raphaelites', 'Natural History in the Green Heart of Umbria', 'Temples and Gardens of Japan' and 'Birds and Natural History of New Zealand'.

For a copy of our free brochure please contact: The Marketing and Publicity Office, School of Continuing Studies, The University of Birmingham, Edgbaston, Birmingham B15 2TT. Tel: 0121 414 5607/7259

Study Tours and Learning Holidays Abroad

■ ■ ■ ■

April 1998

☐ ☐ ☐ ☐

2–18 April
2836 Seychelles: natural
history and conservation
in a tropical paradise £3200
Field Studies Council Overseas
Seychelles

4–10 April
2837 Walking in the Charente £430
2838 Painting £450
2839 French for Francophiles £495
Chateau L'Age Baston
La Rochefoucauld, France

4–19 April
2840 Quest for a quetzal:
Mayan culture and
natural history in
Guatemala £2200
Field Studies Council Overseas
Guatemala

6–16 April
2841 Sicilia antiqua £AFD
Andante Travels *Palermo, Agricento,
Syracuse (Sicily)*

8–15 April
2842 Easter on Guernsey:
flowers and landscapes
in the Channel Islands £770
Field Studies Council Overseas ·
Guernsey

9–17 April
2843 Ice cold in Svalbard: an
Arctic archipelago in
spring £1980
Field Studies Council Overseas
Svalbard, Norway

9–18 April
2844 French £AFD*
Les Taillades Language Studies
Gaillac, France
*also 7/14 day courses.

9–19 April
2845 Cyprus: flowers in the
landscape £1030
Field Studies Council Overseas
Cyprus

11–17 April
2846 Walking in the Charente £430
2847 Painting £450
2848 French for Francophiles £495
Chateau L'Age Baston
La Rochefoucauld, France

11–18 April
2849 Irish language – all levels £100*
Oideas Gael *County Donegal,
Southern Ireland*
**Tuition fees. Details available for
accommodation options.*

12–18 April
2850 Painting in France £222**/316*
Le Petit Bois
ARCA Gleu Renaze, France
*per artist.
**per non-painting guest.

14–23 April
2851 Bulgaria £AFD
Andante Travels *Plovdiv, Venko
Turnovo, Sofia (Bulgaria)*

14–24 April
2852 Italian (all levels) £AFD
2853 Architecture in Florence £AFD
British Institute of Florence *Italy
Accommodation arranged in
Florentine homes or pensioni.*

16–19 April
2854   Nancy: Rococo to Art
        Nouveau   £AFD
Univ Birmingham *Nancy, France*

18–24 April
2855   Walking in the Charente   £430
2856   Painting   £450
2857   French for Francophiles   £495
Chateau L'Age Baston
La Rochefoucauld, France

18–25 April
2858   Arran adventures:
        geology, archaeology and
        natural history of a
        Scottish island   £540
Field Studies Council Overseas *Arran, Scotland*

19–25 April
2859   Painting in France   £222**/316*
Le Petit Bois
ARCA Gleu Renaze, France
*per artist.
**per non-painting guest.

20–26 April
2860   Palladian villas, Veneto   £AFD
Andante Travels *Bassano del Grappa (Italy)*

22–26 April
2861   Beyond the bulbfields: a
        wider perspective of
        Dutch horticulture   £AFD
Univ Birmingham *The Netherlands*

25 April–2 May
2862   Walking in the Charente   £430
2863   Painting   £450
2864   French for Francophiles   £495
Chateau L'Age Baston
La Rochefoucauld, France

26 April–2 May
2865   Painting in France   £222**/316*
Le Petit Bois
ARCA Gleu Renaze, France
*per artist.
**per non-painting guest.

26 April–10 May
2866   Flowers of Andalucia:
        Serranía de Ronda and
        Costa de la Luz   £1350
Field Studies Council Overseas
Andalucia, Spain

27 April–3 May
2867   Malta   £AFD
Andante Travels *Valletta (Malta)*

27 April–22 May
2868   Italian (all levels)   £AFD
2869   Florentine Renaissance   £AFD
2870   Drawing   £AFD
2871   Italian cooking   £AFD
British Institute of Florence *Italy Accommodation arranged in Florentine homes or pensioni.*

■   ■   ■   ■

May 1998

□   □   □   □

1–12 May
2872   Central Anatolia   £AFD
Andante Travels *Ankara, Goreme, Konya, Antalya (Turkey)*

2–9 May
2873   Art in Florence   £AFD
British Institute of Florence *Italy Accommodation arranged in Florentine homes or pensioni.*

3–9 May
2874   Painting in France   £222**/316*
Le Petit Bois
ARCA Gleu Renaze, France
*per artist.
**per non-painting guest.

9–16 May
2875   Islamic Spain   £750
Univ Nottingham *Spain*

9–16 May
2876 Mallorca study tour   £530
Univ Wales, Swansea *Northern Mallorca*

10–16 May
2877 Painting in France   £222**/316*
Le Petit Bois
ARCA Gleu Renaze, France
*per artist.
**per non-painting guest.

10–17 May
2878 Archaeology in the west
of Ireland   £AFD
Univ Birmingham *Galway and Sligo*

10–24 May
2879 Painting in Greece   £1060
Field Studies Council Overseas
Greece

11–22 May
2880 Italian opera   £AFD
British Institute of Florence *Italy*
Accommodation arranged in Florentine homes or pensioni.

14–18 May
2881 Private break in
Barcelona   £AFD
Andante Travels *Barcelona (Spain)*

15–29 May
2882 Petra and beyond: an
archaeological study tour   £1300
Univ Nottingham *Jordan*

17–23 May
2883 Painting in France   £222**/316*
Le Petit Bois
ARCA Gleu Renaze, France
*per artist.
**per non-painting guest.

17–24 May
2884 Business French   £350
Les Taillades Language Studies
Gaillac, France

17–27 May
2885 North Cyprus   £AFD
Andante Travels *Kyrenia, Salamis (N. Cyprus)*

17–31 May
2886 French   £AFD*
Les Taillades Language Studies
Gaillac, France
also 7/14 day courses.

20 May–3 June
2887 The American
southwest: ecology and
geology in California and
Arizona   £1990
Field Studies Council Overseas
California and Arizona, USA

23–29 May
2888 Walking in the Charente   £430
2889 Painting   £450
2890 French for Francophiles   £495
Chateau L'Age Baston *La Rochefoucauld, France*

23–30 May
2891 Apulia   £AFD
Andante Travels *Cisternino (S. Italy)*
2892 Sardinia – the Nuraghi   £AFD
Andante Travels *Nora, Oristano, Oliena (Sardinia)*

23–30 May
2893 Flowers of the Burren:
Ireland's botanical
enigma   £730
Field Studies Council Overseas
Ireland

23–30 May
2894 Western Turkey: historic
sites of ancient Ionia   £865/973
Maryland College *Turkey*
ARCA

23–30 May
2895 Wildflowers of the
Burren   £525
Univ Nottingham *Lisdoonvarna, Co Clare, Ireland*

23 May–1 June
2896 Algonquin in Spring:
maple and moose, birch
and beaver, lake and loon   £1400
Field Studies Council Overseas
Canada

23 May–9 June
2897 Wildlife of Yellowstone
     and Yosemite   £2100
Univ Nottingham *USA*

24–30 May
2898 Palladian villas, Veneto   £AFD
Andante Travels *Bassano del Grappa
(Italy)*

24–30 May
2899 Painting in France   £222**/316*
Le Petit Bois
ARCA Gleu Renaze, France
*per artist.
**per non-painting guest.*

24–31 May
2900 Carthage and Roman
     Tunisia   £AFD
Andante Travels *Tunis, Donglia,
Hammamet (Tunisia)*

24–31 May
2901 Business French   £350
Les Taillades Language Studies
Gaillac, France

25 May–19 June
2902 Italian (all levels)   £AFD
2903 High Renaissance   £AFD
2904 Drawing   £AFD
2905 Italian cooking   £AFD
British Institute of Florence *Italy
Accommodation arranged in
Florentine homes or pensioni.*

26–28 May
2906 Renaissance masters   £AFD
British Institute of Florence *Italy
Accommodation arranged in
Florentine homes or pensioni.*

29 May–1 June
2907 Irish language, all levels   £50*
2908 Cultural hillwalking   £45*
Oideas Gael *County Donegal,
Southern Ireland*
*Tuition fees. Details available for
accommodation options.*

29 May–4 June
2909 Britain and her allies at
     war: Normandy (1944),
     Amiens (1918) and the
     Somme (1916)   £570
Univ Birmingham *Caen, Amiens and
Albert*

30 May–5 June
2910 Walking in the Charente   £430
2911 Painting   £450
2912 French for Francophones   £495
Chateau L'Age Baston *La
Rochefoucauld, France*

31 May–6 June
2913 Painting in France   £222**/316*
Le Petit Bois
ARCA Gleu Renaze, France
*per artist.
**per non-painting guest.*

■   ■   ■   ■

June 1998

□   □   □   □

June
2914 Natural history in the
     green heart of Italy
     (Umbria)   £AFD
Univ Birmingham *Umbria, Italy*

2–9 June
2915 Romanesque Quercy   £AFD
Andante Travels
Beaulieu-sur-Dordogne (France)

2–9 June
2916 Picos de Europa:
     exploring one of
     Europe's last wildlife
     refuges   £860
Field Studies Council Overseas *Picos
de Europa, Spain*

145

2–16 June
2917 Picos de Europa:
exploring one of
Europe's last wildlife
refuges   £1470
Field Studies Council Overseas *Picos de Europa, Spain*

6–7 June
2918 Geology in south-east
Ireland   £AFD
Univ Wales, Swansea *Rosslare, Ireland*

6–12 June
2919 Walking in the Charente   £430
2920 Painting   £450
2921 French for Francophiles   £495
Chateau L'Age Baston *La Rochefoucauld, France*

6–13 June
2922 Mull in midsummer:
otters and eagles   £650
Field Studies Council Overseas *Mull, Scotland*

7–13 June
2923 Painting in France   £222**/316*
Le Petit Bois
ARCA Gleu Renaze, France
**per artist.*
***per non-painting guest.*

10–17 June
2924 Colonsay: wild flowers
and other fascinations of
a Hebridean island   £720
Field Studies Council Overseas
Colonsay, Scotland

13–19 June
2925 Walking in the Charente   £430
2926 Painting   £450
2927 French for Francophiles   £495
Chateau L'Age Baston *La Rochefoucauld, France*

13–20 June
2928 Irish language, all levels   £100*
Oideas Gael *County Donegal, Southern Ireland*
**Tuition fees. Details available for accommodation options.*

13–27 June
2929 Namibian rock art   £AFD
Andante Travels *Namibia*

14–20 June
2930 Painting in France   £222**/316*
Le Petit Bois
ARCA Gleu Renaze, France
**per artist.*
***per non-painting guest.*

14–24 June
2931 French   £AFD*
Les Taillades Language Studies
Gaillac, France
**also 7/14 day courses.*

15–21 June
2932 Ravenna, hills and coast   £AFD
Andante Travels *Brisighella (Italy)*

15–22 June
2933 Piero della Francesca   £AFD
Andante Travels *Sansepoucro, Cortona (Italy)*

18–23 June
2934 Dublin's heritage   £445
Univ Nottingham *Dublin*

20–26 June
2935 Walking in the Charente   £430
2936 Painting   £450
2937 French for Francophiles   £495
Chateau L'Age Baston *La Rochefoucauld, France*

20–27 June
2938 Irish language, all levels   £100*
Oideas Gael *County Donegal, Southern Ireland*
**Tuition fees. Details available for accommodation options.*

20 June–2 July
2939 Carpathian landscapes:
geology, natural history
and castles in Romania   £1380
Field Studies Council Overseas
Romania

20 June–4 July
2940 The High Pyrenees:
flowers, birds and
butterflies £1400
Field Studies Council Overseas
Pyrenees, Spain

21–27 June
2941 Painting in France £222**/316*
Le Petit Bois
ARCA Gleu Renaze, France
*per artist.
**per non-painting guest.

22–28 June
2942 Ravenna, hills and coast £AFD
Andante Travels *Brisighella (Italy)*

22 June–3 July
2943 Italian (all levels) £AFD
2944 Tuscan cities £AFD
British Institute of Florence *Italy*
Accommodation arranged in
Florentine homes or pensioni.

24 June–8 July
2945 The Canadian Rockies:
an ecological exploration £2200
Field Studies Council Overseas
Rockies, Canada

27 June–3 July
2946 Walking in the Charente £430
2947 Painting £450
2948 French for Francophiles £495
Chateau L'Age Baston *La*
Rochefoucauld, France

27 June–4 July
2949 Irish language, all levels £100*
Oideas Gael *County Donegal,*
Southern Ireland
*Tuition fees. Details available for
accommodation options.*

28 June– 4 July
2950 Painting in France £222**/316*
Le Petit Bois
ARCA Gleu Renaze, France
*per artist.
**per non-painting guest.

28 June–4 July
2951 Irish studies £430
2952 Irish humour £430
Summer Academy, Univ College *Cork*

28 June–8 July
2953 Buying a house in France £AFD
Les Taillades Language Studies
Gaillac, France

■ ■ ■ ■

July 1998

□ □ □ □

4–10 July
2954 Walking in the Charente £430
2955 Painting £450
2956 French for Francophiles £495
Chateau L'Age Baston *La*
Rochefoucauld, France

4–11 July
2957 Irish language, all
learning levels £100*
2958 Tapestry weaving £90*
2959 Celtic pottery £90*
Oideas Gael *County Donegal,*
Southern Ireland
*Tuition fees. Details available for
accommodation options.*

5–11 July
2960 Painting in France £222**/316*
Le Petit Bois
ARCA Gleu Renaze, France
*per artist.
**per non-painting guest.

5–11 July
2961 Cork: a writer's
landscape £430
2962 A century of Irish theatre £430
Summer Academy, Univ College *Cork*

6–31 July
2963 Italian (all levels) £AFD
2964 Florentine Renaissance £AFD

6–31 July continued
2965 Drawing £AFD
2966 Italian cooking £AFD
British Institute of Florence *Italy*
Accommodation arranged in
Florentine homes or pensioni.

9–19 July
2967 The Bernese Oberland:
    mountain flowers and
    walking £1280
Field Studies Council Overseas
Switzerland

10–18 July
2968 Medieval Hungary £AFD
Andante Travels *Gellert (Hungary)*

11–17 July
2969 Walking in the Charente £430
2970 Painting £450
2971 French for Francophiles £495
Chateau L'Age Baston *La*
Rochefoucauld, France

11–18 July
2972 Art in Florence £AFD
British Institute of Florence *Italy*
Accommodation arranged in
Florentine homes or pensioni.

11–18 July
2973 Irish language, all
    learning levels £100*
2974 Cultural hillwalking in
    Donegal Highlands £80*
2975 Tapestry weaving £90*
2976 Marine painting summer
    school £90*
Oideas Gael *County Donegal,*
Southern Ireland
*Tuition fees. Details available for
accommodation options.

11–21 July
2977 West Iceland wildlife:
    the natural history of
    Snaefellsnes and
    Westfjord £1450
Field Studies Council Overseas
Iceland

12–18 July
2978 Painting in France £222**/316*
Le Petit Bois
ARCA Gleu Renaze, France
* per artist.
** per non-painting guest.

12–18 July
2979 Celtic civilisation £430
Summer Academy, Univ College *Cork*

12–19 July
2980 Local history, art and
    architecture: Albi and the
    Cathars £AFD
Les Taillades Language Studies
Gaillac, France

14–21 July
2981 Roman Provence £AFD
Andante Travels *St. Remy de*
Provence (France)

18–24 July
2982 Walking in the Charente £430
2983 Painting £450
2984 French for Francophiles £495
Chateau L'Age Baston *La*
Rochefoucauld, France

18–25 July
2985 The Isles of Scilly:
    landscape and
    archaeology £750
Field Studies Council Overseas *Scilly*
Isles

18–25 July
2986 Irish language, all
    learning levels £100*
2987 Cultural hillwalking in
    Donegal Highlands £80*
Oideas Gael *County Donegal,*
Southern Ireland
*Tuition fees. Details available for
accommodation options.

18–27 July
2988 Megalithic Brittany £AFD
Andante Travels *Vannes,*
Perros-Guirec (France)

18–27 July
2989 The Outer Hebrides:
from Butt of Lewis to
Sound of Harris £950
Field Studies Council Overseas *Outer
Hebrides, Scotland*

19–25 July
2990 Painting in France £222**/316*
Le Petit Bois
ARCA Gleu Renaze, France
per artist.
***per non-painting guest.**

19–25 July
2991 Folklore and cultural
heritage of Ireland £430
Summer Academy, Univ College *Cork*

19–29 July
2992 French £AFD*
Les Taillades Language Studies
Gaillac, France
also 7/14 day courses.

20–31 July
2993 Renaissance history £AFD
British Institute of Florence *Italy
Accommodation arranged in
Florentine homes or pensioni.*

21–29 July
2994 Czech Republic, art and
architecture £AFD
Andante Travels *Prague, Telc, Cesky,
Krumlov (Czech Rep.)*

22 July–12 August
2995 Where Asia wears a
smile: a wildlife journey
through the Philippines £2600
Field Studies Council Overseas
Philippines

25–31 July
2996 Walking in the Charente £430
2997 Painting £450
2998 French for Francophiles £495
Chateau L'Age Baston *La
Rochefoucauld, France*

25–31 July
2999 Irish history and
archaeology £395
3000 Georgian Ireland £395
Summer Academy, St Patrick's
College *Maynooth*

25 July–1 August
3001 Irish language, all
learning levels £100*
3002 Irish language and
culture summer school £115*
Oideas Gael *County Donegal,
Southern Ireland*
*Tuition fees. Details available for
accommodation options.*

26 July–1 August
3003 Painting in France £222**/316*
Le Petit Bois
ARCA Gleu Renaze, France
per artist.
***per non-painting guest.**

28 July–6 August
3004 Lithuania: foraging for
Fungi £1300
Field Studies Council Overseas
Lithuania

30 July–9 August
3005 French £AFD*
Les Taillades Language Studies
Gaillac, France
also 7/14 day courses.

■   ■   ■   ■

August 1998

☐   ☐   ☐   ☐

Mid-August
3006   Human origins in the
       African Savannah   £AFD
Andante Travels *Southern Africa*

1–7 August
3007   Walking in the Charente   £430
3008   Painting   £450
3009   French for Francophiles   £495
Chateau L'Age Baston *La*
Rochefoucauld, France

1–7 August
3010   History of Irish art   £395
3011   Celtic Christianity   £395
Summer Academy, St Patrick's
College *Maynooth*

1–8 August
3012   Archaeology summer
       school   £90*
3013   Irish language at all
       learning levels   £100*
Oideas Gael *County Donegal,*
Southern Ireland
Tuition fees. Details available for
accommodation options.

2–8 August
3014   Painting in France   £222**/316*
Le Petit Bois
ARCA Gleu Renaze, France
*per artist.
**per non-painting guest.*

3–8 August
3015   Eastern Germany – art
       history   £AFD
Andante Travels *Dresden, Meissen*

3–14 August
British Institute summer school
3016   Italian (all levels)   £AFD
3017   Italian opera   £AFD
3018   Art in Siena   £AFD
British Institute of Florence *Massa*
Marittima, Italy
Accommodation arranged.

8–14 August
3019   Walking in the Charente   £430
3020   Painting   £450
3021   French for Francophiles   £495
Chateau L'Age Baston *La*
Rochefoucauld, France

8–15 August
3022   Manx magic: marine
       biology and naturla
       history on the Isle of
       Man   £680
Field Studies Council Overseas *Isle of*
Man

8–15 August
3023   Irish language at all
       learning levels   £100*
Oideas Gael *County Donegal,*
Southern Ireland
Tuition fees. Details available for
accommodation options.

8–16 August
3024   In the steps of the
       Plantagenets   £735
Univ Nottingham *Loire Valley, France*

9–15 August
3025   Painting in France   £222**/316*
Le Petit Bois
ARCA Gleu Renaze, France
*per artist.
**per non-painting guest.*

9–19 August
3026   French   £AFD*
Les Taillades Language Studies
Gaillac, France
also 7/14 day courses.

15–21 August
3027   Walking in the Charente   £430
3028   Painting   £450
3029   French and French
       country cooking   £645
Chateau L'Age Baston *La*
Rochefoucauld, France

15–22 August
3030 Irish language at all
learning levels £100*
Oideas Gael *County Donegal,
Southern Ireland*
*Tuition fees. Details available for
accommodation options.*

16–22 August
3031 Painting in France £222**/316*
Le Petit Bois
ARCA Gleu Renaze, France
per artist.
**per non-painting guest.*

17–28 August
3032 Two-centre vacation
course – Italian (all levels) £AFD
British Institute of Florence *Massa
Marittima and Florence, Italy
Accommodation arranged.*

20–30 August
3033 French £AFD*
Les Taillades Language Studies
Gaillac, France
also 7/14 day courses.

22–28 August
3034 Walking in the Charente £430
3035 Painting £450
3036 French and French
country cooking £645
Chateau L'Age Baston *La
Rochefoucauld, France*

22–29 August
3037 Irish language at all
learning levels £100*
3038 Traditional dances of
Ireland £70*
Oideas Gael *County Donegal,
Southern Ireland*
*Tuition fees. Details available for
accommodation options.*

23–29 August
3039 Painting in France £222**/316*
Le Petit Bois
ARCA Gleu Renaze, France
per artist.
**per non-painting guest.*

29 August–4 September
3040 Walking in the Charente £430
3041 Painting £450
3042 French for Francophiles £495
Chateau L'Age Baston *La
Rochefoucauld, France*

30 August–5 September
3043 Painting in France £222**/316*
Le Petit Bois
ARCA Gleu Renaze, France
per artist.
**per non-painting guest.*

30 August–6 September
3044 French and wine £AFD
Les Taillades Language Studies
Gaillac, France

30 August–9 September
3045 French £AFD*
Les Taillades Language Studies
Gaillac, France
also 7/14 day courses.

■　　■　　■　　■

September 1998

☐　　☐　　☐　　☐

Late September
3046 Bushman rock art of S.
Africa £AFD
Andante Travels *South Africa*

1–5 September
3047 The Dante course £AFD
British Institute of Florence *Italy
Accommodation arranged in
Florentine homes or pensioni.*

1–25 September
3048 Italian (all levels) £AFD
3049 Florentine Renaissance £AFD
3050 Italian cooking £AFD
British Institute of Florence *Italy
Accommodation arranged in
Florentine homes or pensioni.*

4–13 September
3051   Temples and gardens of
     Japan   £1975
Univ Birmingham *Japan*

4–22 September
3052   Birding in Bolivia: birds of
     the mountains, lakes and
     forests   £3000
Field Studies Council Overseas
Bolivia

5–11 September
3053   Walking in the Charente   £430
3054   Painting   £450
3055   French for Francophiles   £495
Chateau L'Age Baston *La
Rochefoucauld, France*

5–12 September
3056   Art in Florence   £AFD
British Institute of Florence *Italy
Accommodation arranged in
Florentine homes or pensioni.*

5–12 September
3057   Carcassonne and the
     Cathars   £AFD
Le Cour du Blé *Carcassonne, France*

6–12 September
3058   Painting in France   £222**/316*
Le Petit Bois
ARCA Gleu Renaze, France
per artist.
**per non-painting guest.*

7–13 September
3059   Tarquinia and the
     Etruscans   £AFD
Andante Travels *S. Martino in Umino
(Italy)*
3060   Altamira and cave
     paintings of N. Spain   £AFD
Andante Travels *Santillana del Mar
(Spain)*
3061   Cave paintings in the
     Dordogne   £AFD
Andante Travels *Les Eyzies (France)*

11–13 September
3062   Traditional dances of
     Ireland   £30*
3063   Learn to play the
     bodhrán   £30*
Oideas Gael *County Donegal,
Southern Ireland*
**Tuition fees. Details available for
accommodation options.*

11–15 September
3064   George Sand study tour,
     France   £AFD
Maryland College *France
ARCA*

12–18 September
3065   Walking in the Charente   £430
3066   Painting   £450
3067   French for Francophiles   £495
Chateau L'Age Baston *La
Rochefoucauld, France*

12–19 September
3068   Carcassonne and the
     Cathars   £AFD
Le Cour du Blé *Carcassonne, France*

12–22 September
3069   Ancient Morocco   £AFD
Andante Travels *Tangier, Fez, Rabat,
Marrakech*

13–19 September
3070   Painting in France   £222**/316*
Le Petit Bois
ARCA Gleu Renaze, France
per artist.
**per non-painting guest.*

13–20 September
3071   Local history, art and
     architecture: Albi and the
     Cathars   £AFD
Les Taillades Language Studies
Gaillac, France

13–27 September
3072   French   £AFD*
Les Taillades Language Studies
Gaillac, France
**also 7/14 day courses.*

14–18 September
3073 Villas and gardens   £AFD
British Institute of Florence *Italy*
Accommodation arranged in
Florentine homes or pensioni.

14–25 September
3074 Italian opera   £AFD
British Institute of Florence *Italy*
Accommodation arranged in
Florentine homes or pensioni.

18–26 September
3075 Ancient Catalunya   £AFD
Andante Travels *Girona and*
Tarragona (Spain)

19–25 September
3076 Walking in the Charente   £430
3077 Painting   £450
3078 French for Francophiles   £495
Chateau L'Age Baston *La*
Rochefoucauld, France

19–26 September
3079 Carcassonne and the
      Cathars   £AFD
Le Cour du Blé *Carcassonne, France*

19 September–3 October
3080 The archaeology of
      Aegean Turkey   £790
Univ Nottingham *Turkey*

20–26 September
3081 Painting in France   £222**/316*
Le Petit Bois
ARCA Gleu Renaze, France
**per artist.*
***per non-painting guest.*

23–27 September
3082 The genesis of modern
      art 1879–1945   £370
Univ Nottingham *Paris*

24 September–8 October
3083 Colour in the American
      fall: natural history and
      photography in the
      White Mountains   £1730
Field Studies Council Overseas *New*
England, USA

26 September–2 October
3084 Walking in the Charente   £430
3085 Painting   £450
3086 French for Francophiles   £495
Chateau L'Age Baston *La*
Rochefoucauld, France

26 September–3 October
3087 Carcassonne and the
      Cathars   £AFD
Le Cour du Blé *Carcassonne, France*

27 September–3 October
3088 Painting in France   £222**/316*
Le Petit Bois
ARCA Gleu Renaze, France
**per artist.*
***per non-painting guest.*

28 September–6 October
3089 Great abbeys of central
      Italy/Rome   £AFD
Andante Travels *Tivoli and S. Donato*
val Comino (Italy)

28 September–8 October
3090 Autumn in Andalucia:
      southern Spain and
      Doñana National Park   £1320
Field Studies Council Overseas
Andalucia, Spain

28 September–23 October
3091 Italian (all levels)   £AFD
3092 Florentine Renaissance   £AFD
3093 Drawing   £AFD
3094 Italian cooking   £AFD
British Institute of Florence *Italy*
Accommodation arranged in
Florentine homes or pensioni.

ORDER FORM
October 1998 - March 1999
Published August 1998

price £4.95 post free in UK
(Overseas airmail £8.00; Overseas surface mail £6.50 sterling)

Please send me   copy/copies of
TIME TO LEARN **October 1998 - March 1999**

☐ Payment of £ .... .enclosed (cheques payable to NIACE)
☐ Please debit my credit card (Visa, Delta, Mastercard, Eurocard) number

☐☐☐☐ ☐☐☐☐ ☐☐☐☐ ☐☐☐☐

Expiry date: ☐☐ ☐☐

Send with payment to:
Publications Sales, NIACE
21 De Montfort Street, Leicester LE1 7GE

OR, take this completed form to your bookseller to order on your behalf

Name: _____

Address: _____

_____

_____

_____

Trade orders to: Central Books Ltd., 99 Wallis Road, London E9 5LN
(Tel: 0181 986 4854; Fax: 0181 533 5821)

Subject Index

The numbers listed in this index refer to the individual numbers assigned to each learning holiday: *they are not page numbers*. To guide you, the learning holidays numbered from 1 to 369 are being held during April 1998; 370 to 889 during May 1998; 890 to 1310 in June 1998; 1311 to 1966 in July, 1998; 1967 to 2540 in August 1998 and 2541 to 2835 in September 1998. Numbers 2836 to 3094 cover learning holidays and study tours abroad.

167